INSIDE
THE HOUSE

INSIDE THE HOUSE

BY DANIEL RAPOPORT

★

★ ★

*An irreverent guided tour
through the House of Representatives,
from the days of Adam Clayton Powell
to those of Peter Rodino*

FOLLETT PUBLISHING COMPANY *CHICAGO*

Dick West's UPI column is reprinted with his permission.

Library of Congress Catalog Card Number: 74-77810
ISBN: 0-695-80486-3

First Printing

To Maxine

ACKNOWLEDGMENTS

So MANY PEOPLE contributed their time, thoughts and knowledge to the writing of this book that it would be futile to try to list them here. Some are identified in the book by their own words and to them go my thanks. But there are others—mentioned either only in passing or not at all—whose assistance was invaluable and whom I would like to cite by name.

A number of present and former congressional staffers, not all of whom view the House as I do, were kind enough to provide me with essential information and background on the workings of Capitol Hill. They include Joe Bartlett, Richard Conlon, Gary Hymel, William Maloni, Paul Miltich, Julian Morrison, Peter Stockton, John Sullivan, Mark Talisman, William Vaughan, Robert Wichser and the staffs of the House Armed Services Committee, Rep. F. Edwards Hébert and Rep. Benjamin Rosenthal.

For the same reasons I am indebted to such outside observers of Congress as David Cohen and Fred Wertheimer of Common Cause, Richard Cook, former Deputy Assistant to the President for Legislative Affairs, my brother Paul, and Jean Cahn and Herbert O. Reid, two of the lawyers who represented the late Adam Clayton Powell in his suit against the House.

Supplying me with facts, recollections and assessments, as well as useful suggestions, were a number of reporters and ex-reporters, among them many of my former UPI colleagues, in particular Mike Feinsilber, and also Con Eklund, Robert Novak, and Leo Rennert.

And it is no exaggeration to say that the book would not have been possible without Frank Eleazer, who taught me most of what I know about the House and about reporting.

I am grateful to John Hess and Denise DeClue of Follett for helping me bring a rambling discourse into some kind of focus, to *Congressional Quarterly* for permitting me to use its superb research facilities and to Barbara Crandall for deciphering my copy and flawlessly typing it into manuscript form.

Finally, thanks to my wife Maxine for loaning me her innate editorial sense as well as for transcribing more taped newsman-politician interviews than any human being ought to endure and to Victoria, Andy and Adam for putting up with half a father during the writing of this book.

DANIEL RAPOPORT

Washington, D.C.
Dec. 10, 1974

PREFACE

IN THE SPRING and summer of 1974 America discovered the House of Representatives. The prospective impeachment of Richard Nixon drew the full force of the media on to the House Judiciary Committee, and in time the public was seeing, hearing and reading about people with names like Rodino, Wiggins, Cohen and Jordan. The American people also learned that House members were usually articulate, frequently thoughtful, occasionally eloquent and just as interesting as senators, whom they knew much better.

Americans all over the country were let in on a secret that I myself and a few other House buffs had held for years: the House can be an exciting place. That doesn't mean it is always a nice place. It has its share of nasty and mediocre members and sometimes they prevail. But it has its worthy members too and now and then they win out. It rarely is a dull place. There are just too many egocentric, extroverted and ambitious politicians around for tameness ever to set in. For a newsman like myself it was the best beat in Washington.

As a reporter for United Press International, I spent ten years covering the House and hardly any time covering the Senate. The first and one of the only times I went over there professionally I ran into two senators wrestling in the hallway. I thought at the time that it made a good story but that it was an odd way to legislate.

Yet that impromptu match in 1964 between Strom Thurmond and Ralph Yarborough made front pages all over the country. Over the years I found that even when senators were talking instead of wrestling, stories about them got better play than stories about the House and House members. That used to bother reporters like me who covered the House as well as the congressmen we wrote about.

I suppose that is one of the main points I want to make in this book: that until impeachment hearings came along, few people outside Washington—and not nearly enough people there—paid attention to the House. But the House is important; its members make decisions that profoundly affect all of our lives. It is also an entertaining place, peopled with some highly capable and colorful men and women. With this in mind, I have tried to describe the House in terms of individuals and events rather than as an "institution," as a flesh and blood community instead of as an abstract entity.

Besides members this book is about the people who work for the House and a little about outsiders, like lobbyists and newsmen, who make a living out of it. I have written from the vantage point of my observations, which means the book roughly incorporates a period of about a dozen years, from 1963 through 1974. Those were tumultuous years for the nation and for the House as well. I have not, however, attempted to present a complete account of even that time span. Some of the major developments of the period are dealt with; others are not. I concentrated on those incidents, trends and people that I, as a reporter, covered and therefore knew best. I also sought out those characteristics which I believe reflect the nature of the House.

There is more here about Democrats than Republicans. That is because Democrats have been running the House uninterruptedly since January 5, 1955, and no matter how dull and poor a job they have done of it (and frequently they did both), they were in charge and thus had more to say about what went on there than did the Republicans.

CONTENTS

INSIDE
THE HOUSE

1

Their Finest Hour

THE BIG MILITARY jet transport touched down at Andrews Air Force Base shortly before noon. Barring an unforeseen hitch, they would make it.

The plane taxied to the terminal, rolled to a stop and opened its door. A dozen or so passengers scrambled down the steps and into a waiting bus. Within moments they were skimming along the Suitland Parkway in suburban Maryland on their way to the Capitol.

Fifteen minutes later the members of the House of Representatives delegation to the NATO Parliamentarians' Conference rushed into the House chamber and answered the quorum call then in process.

The congressmen should have been in Ankara, Turkey. They had landed there on Friday, October 19, 1973, and were readying themselves for the meeting, an annual affair which regularly draws the serious congressional student of Atlantic policy as well as the out-and-out junketeer. Instead they were back in Washington, the result of a quick decision made Sunday. They awoke that morning to news of

3

the "Saturday Night Massacre." President Nixon had fired Archibald Cox, the special prosecutor he had appointed to investigate the Watergate cover-up and the related crimes it had spawned or unearthed. The cataclysmic reaction was felt even in Turkey. Cries of impeachment were sounded in the House. And now they were coming from people besides longtime Nixon critics such as Bella Abzug. Nor could the threats of an impeachment vote be dismissed as rhetoric. Under House rules any member was privileged to rise on any day and demand that the House vote to impeach the president of the United States.

It had been 105 years since the House had cast its first and only vote on impeaching a president and thirty-seven years since it had voted on impeaching anybody.* "We had no way of knowing whether a member was going to exercise the privilege," Paul Findley, Illinois Republican and member of the delegation, later recalled. "We weren't about to take the chance of missing the most important vote of our careers."

As it turned out, there was no vote that Monday. Nor was the House ever faced with voting on whether Richard Nixon should be removed from office. But during the next nine months the House moved inexorably toward such a vote, toward a decision that would certainly have gone against the president. Only Nixon's resignation on August 9, 1974—brought about in part because of the sentiment in the House—spared him the ignominy of impeachment.

---

* Coincidentally, the House impeached Andrew Johnson—at least ostensibly—because he too had fired one of his appointees, Secretary of War Edwin Stanton. Although the rift between Johnson and Congress had its roots in differences over Reconstruction policy, the House formally impeached him on February 24, 1868, for dismissing Stanton without congressional approval, as required by the recently passed Tenure of Office Act. The Supreme Court subsequently upheld Johnson's view that the act was unconstitutional. The last person to be impeached by the House was U.S. District Court Judge Halsted Ritter of Florida, in 1936.

The prospect of impeachment was not a thought that came easily to the House. Only a few weeks before the Saturday Night Massacre, even when the Watergate scandal seemed likely to end in the Oval Office of the president, it was heresy to mention impeachment. Conservative Republican Earl Landgrebe of Indiana forced the House to adjourn one day in order to block liberal Republican Paul McCloskey from discussing the possibility of impeachment. Landgrebe was Nixon's most extreme and ludicrous defender in the House. Nevertheless, many more rational members thought McCloskey had exhibited poor taste. To them, impeachment was a charge flung out by left wing Democrats and similar longtime Nixon haters.

The firing of Cox changed all that. The president had torpedoed the Watergate investigation; Congress had to react. The House establishment took the first tentative steps toward an impeachment investigation. It wasn't to be an out-and-out investigation, but rather a preliminary inquiry to determine whether impeachment proceedings were necessary. (Somewhere along the line the distinction became blurred and the preliminary inquiry evolved into the impeachment proceedings.)

But before an investigation could begin, agreement had to be reached on who the investigators would be. The Judiciary Committee was the likely unit, but not everybody was happy with that likelihood. Nixon supporters contended the panel was loaded with too many Democratic liberals. Some Nixon critics were unsure about the committee's new chairman, Peter Rodino. Could the relatively obscure, machine politician from Newark, New Jersey, handle the awesome task? A clamor arose for creation of a special committee to conduct the probe.

But the Democratic leadership, as Majority Leader Thomas (Tip) O'Neill put it, decided to "let Peter handle it." Rodino, the country was to learn, proved to be the right man for the job. At critical points he made the correct decisions. His hiring of former Assistant Attorney General John Doar as counsel for the inquiry assured that the legal staff work would be sound, that standing behind its conclusions would be a man of unimpeachable integrity. Despite later press complaints that the investigation was faltering, that the fragile bipartisan coalition was breaking apart, Rodino brought the investigation to an orderly and, considering the respectable number of Republicans* that voted for the articles of impeachment, nonpartisan end.

Committee members deservedly won plaudits six days in late July when live television recorded their debates and votes on the impeachment articles. Newspapers throughout the country heaped editorial praise on the committee for what was described as the dignity and thoughtfulness they brought to a task which for many was politically difficult and spiritually painful.

Northern liberal viewers saw that southern conservatives like Democrats James Mann of South Carolina and Walter Flowers of Alabama and Republican Caldwell Butler of Virginia understood the meaning of civil liberties and were willing to risk political retribution in their behalf. Conservatives in the country discovered that ultraliberals like Don Edwards of California and Robert Kastenmeier of Wisconsin were not wild men, but civilized, calm proponents of a respectable philosophy. And everyone recognized the moral agony that Republicans such as Thomas

---

* Seven Republicans joined all twenty-one Democrats in voting 28 to 10 for the second article, charging Nixon with abusing his presidential powers. The first article, charging obstruction of justice in the Watergate cover-up, passed by a vote of 27 to 11, with the aye votes including six Republicans. The final article, accusing Nixon of contempt of Congress for refusing to comply with committee subpoenas, drew only two Republican supporters and passed by the narrow margin of 21 to 17.

Railsback and Robert McClory of Illinois were going through in casting their vote for impeachment.

Yet the committee's performance was not unflawed. In weighing the evidence, Nixon defenders and even some of those who eventually voted for his impeachment, too casually accepted his refusal to produce additional tapes. Charles Wiggins of California, the most capable of the president's advocates, exhibited tortuous legal reasoning to reject the notion that one should draw an "adverse inference" from Nixon's defiance of the subpoenas. Right up to the point of voting, Republicans on and off the committee proclaimed that the "smoking pistol" still had not been placed in Nixon's hands. Few were willing to address themselves to the proposition that the pistol might well be among the withheld tapes.

On August 5, 1974, the president himself admitted that the evidence linking him to the cover-up—the photograph, so to speak, of him firing the pistol—could be found in the taped conversation of June 23, 1972, one of those that the committee had subpoenaed but had never received. Although it was too late to change their votes on the impeachment articles, the holdout Republicans signed the committee's report, which called for Nixon's impeachment.

One could feel little sympathy for two crestfallen Republicans, Edward Hutchinson of Michigan and David Dennis of Indiana. The president had "deceived" him complained Hutchinson. Why, if he had known of the June 23 tape, he would never have voted to exonerate Nixon. Dennis tried to philosophically dismiss the betrayal he felt by remarking that it wasn't the first time a "client had lied to me." (So much for the administration argument that it was the Democrats who had forsaken their obligation to sit as unbiased judges. Dennis considered himself the president's lawyer.)

Impeachment and Watergate finally destroyed President Nixon; it also brought the House to the attention of millions of American citizens who never before had noticed it. It should not have taken a monumental political tragedy to bring about recognition for the House. The impact of its decisions has been affecting our daily lives for years.

The House has determined who among our young should live and who should die, who should bear the heaviest burden in paying taxes and how much should be spent on educating our children, ministering to our elderly and caring for our poor.

The House kept the war in Vietnam going almost two years after the Senate was ready to drop it. Whether the House is to be commended or denounced for that depends on your view of the war. But less defensible is what the House did in 1967 when Congress extended and revised the nation's draft laws. That reshaping of our conscription system produced one significant result: poor and lower-middle-class youths made up a disproportionate share of the 55,000 American war deaths. The dominant influence in that legislative revamping of the draft was the House Armed Services Committee.

If you're a liberal who believed that the quickest and most effective path to Lyndon Johnson's Great Society was through the U.S. Treasury, compare the annual House and Senate appropriations of the past decade for education, health and antipoverty programs. The House figures were usually lower, sometimes by hundreds of millions of dollars. Often the differences were split down the middle but more often than not, the "compromise" leaned toward the House's lower appropriation. The cumulative effect was a shortfall of billions of dollars.

Conservatives as well as liberals have been unhappy with the amounts of money we provide the poor, one believing it's too much, the other, too little. Neither likes the methods by which it is doled out, one considering it too loose, the other too demeaning. The same groups, again for different reasons, think our tax system is discriminatory. Few of these Americans, however, thought of complaining to Wilbur Mills and the House Ways and Means Committee, although, as the Washington press corps had been claiming for years, they were "powerful," "influential" and had the last word on welfare, taxes and trade.

If you believe children in public schools should begin their day with a prayer, you can blame the House for effectively shooting down a proposed constitutional amendment that would have overridden the Supreme Court's decision banning prayers. And if you watch television or listen to the radio, you can thank—or curse—the House, which in 1964 bludgeoned the Federal Communications Commission into dropping plans for cutting down the number of commercials broadcast.

Aside from lobbyists, administration officials and some newsmen, hardly anyone appreciates the significance of House actions such as these. To a good part of the country —including some columnists and editorial writers who ought to know better—the House is the "lower body" while the Senate is the "upper body." The term annoys representatives to no end, first because it's incorrect and, secondly, because it goes hand in hand with the dull, low life image that the House has portrayed to the country. (Constitutionally and historically, one body is as important as the other. Ironically, the terms apparently originate from the pre-Capitol days of the Republic, when the Senate was relegated to less desirable space in an attic-like area.) Sadly for the House, the basic reason for its drab image stems not from performance but from the dimensions of the animal.

The House is still too large to personalize. No matter how many stars infiltrate the place, the overwhelming majority will be reduced to faceless names. To almost all

Americans and most newspapermen the 435 members of the House constitute an amorphous, uninteresting mass, a glob of spilled Jell-O slithering and sliding from left to right on a shaky table.

People think of the Senate as one hundred individuals. They see the House as an entity. The word "Senate" evokes memories of American history—stirring debate and towering men. The word "House," as used when talking about the House of Representatives, always seems to come out sounding like a great big galoot, who occasionally burns with a touch of emotion but more often simply slogs—or refuses to slog—blandly from one task to another. The word "Congress" connotes the same kind of image to a listener. Both words drip with dullness. Both suggest something that is big, cumbersome, a little slow mentally and very slow physically.

Years ago sports cartoonist Willard Mullin of the old *New York World Telegram* created symbolic figures for all of the major league baseball clubs. For the Giants, my favorite team, Mullin would draw a huge oaf in a gray baseball uniform, a figure shaped like a Macy's parade balloon, a great round body, topped off by a pin head and a face with a slightly dopey look. He was the kind of guy that almost everybody pushed around (which, unfortunately for me and the Giants, almost everybody did when I was growing up). That would be the perfect cartoon character to represent the House. "Whoever heard of a charismatic Congress?" Sen. Lloyd Bentsen once asked. Who would ever think of a charismatic House?

The "uncharismatic" Gerald Ford is the first president of the United States who could truly be called a man of the House of Representatives. Seventeen other presidents have served in the House and one (James Polk) rose to Speaker, an achievement that escaped Ford. But Ford is the only one who has never run for any other statewide or federal elective office. As far as we know he has never seriously aspired to any other political office and was never mentioned as a presidential possibility during the twenty-five years of public life he recorded before becoming president. He came out of the navy in 1945, practiced law in Grand Rapids, Michigan, for three years and in 1948 won election to the House from a heavily Republican district by ousting the isolationist incumbent in the GOP primary. For the next 24 years and 339 days he devoted himself to the House, the Republican party and his family, frequently in that order.

On December 6, 1973, Chief Justice Warren Burger swore in Ford as Richard Nixon's choice to succeed the departed and disgraced Spiro Agnew as vice-president. Nixon staged the White House introduction ceremony with all the suspense and good taste of a "Queen for a Day" performance. But the television cameras did pick up one interesting happening. When Ford stepped through the door to stand before the audience that had been assembled, House members who were on hand let out with an undignified but characteristically House-style burst of cheers and rebel yells. "It's one of ours" was written all over their beaming faces.

Less than eight months later, in a considerably more somber setting, Burger swore in Ford to succeed the disgraced and departed Richard Nixon. In no time at all Ford was in the throes of a near-perfect honeymoon with Congress, the press and the voters. The media, which for years had dismissed him as unimaginative, plodding and overly conservative, now told us that he was doing just fine and could well make one hell of a president. He had brought back to the White House qualities that had been missing from there for too long—honesty, plain speaking and openness. The imperial presidency was once again the unpretentious presidency.

Within two weeks after taking office, Ford the plodder had become the odds-on-favorite to win the presidency on his own right in 1976. To someone who had watched Ford, the old Ford, the change in the appraisal of him was remarkable and amusing. During those ten years no one ever thought of Gerald Ford as presidential timber, even though he held positions in Congress and at party conventions that attracted about as much notice as a Republican could hope to attract during Democratic years. I cannot recall hearing anyone—House member, staff aide or newsman—suggest Ford as a possible GOP presidential nominee. Not even as one of the field in the preconvention sweepstakes. I vaguely remember someone thinking aloud that he might just make a passable vice-presidential candidate and perhaps ought to be considered a dark horse choice for that normally lackluster office.

No one thought of Gerald Ford as a national leader because when you came right down to it he wasn't terribly impressive, a fact of life that even his admirers would admit. A nice guy, sure. A hard worker, Lord knows, yes. But rarely did they describe him as brilliant, canny, Machiavellian or charismatic—those familiar Washington adjectives applied to politicians on the rise or the make. The conventional view in the Capitol was that Ford stood as the front man for the tough-minded Republican pros who in 1965 had decided to dump garrulous old Charlie Halleck as GOP House leader and replace him with fresh-faced and affable Jerry Ford.

During his nine years as leader, Ford was brushed aside by most of the media as inconsequential or something even less flattering. Lyndon Johnson cracked that Ford had played football too long without a helmet and drew smiles from White House reporters. Those of us who covered the House regularly thought a bit better of him, but not that much better.

He was a mediocre performer on the floor, grabbing at tired clichés and old saws. (How many times did we hear him warn administration opponents that "We must not tie the hands of the president"? How often we despaired as he plunged into another lengthy nautical or sports metaphor, taking us down to the ten-yard line with the clock running out or steering us away from dangerous shoals.) He was anything but fast on the draw in debates and more often than he cared to remember, young Democratic members nicked him during an exchange. We made fun of his diction. (The word judgment, one of his favorites, usually came out with three syllables: "judg-eh-ment.") Most of the time, however, we just took him for granted.

In retrospect I must confess that we were unkind as well as unfair to him. Despite our put down of him, which I feel he must have at least sensed, he remained remarkably accessible, truthful and good-natured with reporters. He was an extremely busy man, but he found time to talk with almost any reporter who made the effort to catch him in his office, on the floor or in his dashes between both.

The first time I sat down with him I had some pleasant surprises. Gone was Babbitt in politics. Before me sat a ruddy, handsome man, dressed in a blue-button-down Oxford shirt with a sensible tie and a dark suit. (An outfit like that would rate comment only in the House where midwestern members seem to lean toward either the drab or the outlandish in dress.) But what struck me most was the change in conversation. Gone were the clichés and hyperbole. Talking to me was an urbane, likable politician who didn't appear to take himself too seriously, a sophisticated practitioner of his art.

We also gave him a bum rap on his professional accomplishments. We didn't quite say that he had done a lousy job; we simply didn't bother to pass any kind of judgment on his record. But afterwards, as I began to think of his nine years as minority leader, I came to the conclusion that Ford had done just about as much as a Republican minority leader could do, particularly when he was as badly outnumbered as Ford usually was. He kept his troops in line without intimidating the followers or holding grudges against the deserters. He worked the old Republican-conservative Democratic coalition to thwart Lyndon Johnson's Great Society when he could and delivered the votes to sustain President Nixon's Vietnam policy and Nixon's vetoes of a Democratic Congress's domestic legislation. And occasionally he broke with the southerners and led his party into an alliance with civil rights forces. In between, he crisscrossed the country attending party functions, speaking in behalf of Republican candidates to the House, spending an average of four nights a week away from home.

Having said all this, I still have reservations about the Ford leadership in the House. It was good, competent leadership, but it certainly wasn't highly skilled or imaginative leadership. He rarely went outside the House to draw expertise or advice. He was primarily a creature of the House, his horizons limited to it.

The qualities of character he brought to the presidency were qualities that ought to have been there in the first place. He quickly shone in that office because of the contrast he offered to his predecessor. But as the country began to discover in the fall of 1974, forthrightness and decency alone were not enough to distinguish a president. A sound intellect and a commitment to independent thought were also required. These are attributes Ford did not particularly demonstrate in the House. Perhaps conditions there did not permit him to exercise those characteristics or permit us to notice them. Observing him as president, we should learn whether he possesses them.

🚩

The American people, and to a certain extent the American media, discovered the House of Representatives in 1973. I had discovered it ten years earlier when United Press International (UPI) assigned me to its five-man staff covering the House. At the time, John McCormack was beginning his first full term as Speaker. A year earlier he had succeeded the late Sam Rayburn, who had first assumed the office in 1940 and who over the years had developed into one of the strongest leaders in House history. McCormack was seventy years old when he became Speaker and his best years were behind him. Although he possessed experience and political skills, McCormack lacked the natural qualities of leadership that Rayburn had brought to the job—qualities which would have been especially welcome in the 1960s when presidents of the United States would successfully attempt to reassert their dominance over Congress.

For the next ten years, McCormack, northern Democrats and a majority of the House followed presidents. So ingrained had the habit become that it continued when Democrat Johnson was replaced by Republican Nixon in 1969 and when McCormack was replaced by Carl Albert in 1971.

The House followed its president in starting wars and ending wars, wars against communists and wars against poverty. On occasion it balked at what a president wanted, but it hardly ever enacted what a president didn't want. Had it hired an advertising agency to zip up its image, the result might have been: "Hi, I'm the House. I was born to follow. Lead me."

The House's record on impeachment was no guarantee that it was entering a new era. Unfortunately, it soon appeared to have been more of an aberration than a turning point. That Judiciary Committee members exercised their own thoughtful judgment, that they reflected national opinion and also helped shape it was due to some unique influences. For once the media and the people were paying attention to the House. Members responded to the country, rather than to internal pressures and mores. The Judiciary Committee, made up entirely of lawyers, has in the past risen to the occasion and demonstrated the best of the legal profession.

With the television cameras gone, with the hordes of reporters turning to other stories, with its own Gerald Ford in the White House, the House in the fall of 1974 seemed too willing to return to its old ways. The November elections, sweeping into office an army of reform-minded freshmen, gave promise to the advent of a new era. Perhaps. But it seemed likely that it would take much more than the swearing-in of seventy-five new Democrats to dismantle the old order. Looming before the activists was a granite institution run by individuals who have been there too long, individuals who have lost the ability to think with freshness and imagination and who instead have luxuriated in the bureaucracy and clubbiness they have created. That is the House I witnessed for the ten years before the impeachment hearings.

2

An Anthropologist's Field Day

THE BEST PLACE to get a feel for House members is to watch them perform on the floor. I use the word "perform" advisedly. I once heard a perceptive woman after her first visit to the spectators' gallery exclaim how fascinated she was by what she had seen. First, it reminded her of a zoo. Then she thought of herself as an anthropologist, observing a strange and unfamiliar culture. She decided, correctly, that an anthropologist would have a field day.

The House floor is a nice place to nap, catch up on paper work and josh around with colleagues. But some members dislike breaking off whatever they're doing in their offices, or in the House gym, to trek over to the Capitol to answer a quorum call or to cast a vote for a bill that could easily have been passed by voice vote. Others don't mind it at all. They enjoy the club-like atmosphere of the floor and of the cloakrooms just off the floor. As in most clubs, some members use the facilities to doze off during quiet periods and with an inordinate number of elderly, there's more napping in the House than one might expect. Then there are the never-waste-a-minute members who always bring along to the floor a stack of mail and memos to work on whenever the debates wane.

The House chamber offers a comfortable setting, much like a nineteenth-century men's club—rows of stuffed leather chairs, thick maroon carpeting, dark polished woodwork, brass spittoons along the back railings. Five vertical aisles slope downward from the rear, dissect a semicircle of ten rows and empty into the chamber's "well," the open area just in front of the Speaker's desk. Below the raised desk of the Speaker sit clerks in two-tiered rows, numbering documents, recording entries into journals and performing the myriad tasks that keep a parliamentary body functioning with an appropriate reverence to officialism and posterity.

Pages dressed in their traditional navy blue pants and white shirts sprint between members and the Speaker's desk, carrying papers bearing motions, proposed amendments and prepared speeches for entry into the *Congressional Record*.

Unlike the Senate, where senators have assigned chairs and desks, there are no desks in the House and members can take almost any of the 448 seats they want. The middle aisle divides the Democratic side (on the east) from the Republican side, but within these two zones members wander about, plopping down wherever they find comfort or companionship. In the third row of both sides are two conference tables, permanently bolted to the floor, which are used as the floor headquarters for party leaders and for committee members managing a bill.

The House chamber occupies the second and third stories of the House wing of the Capitol. To those sitting in the galleries and looking down on the floor, it resembles an arena or a pit.

Depending on when you arrive in the chamber, you will probably have a different impression of what goes on there. Should a tourist stroll in during "general debate" on a bill —a particularly tedious and uneventful period before the amending stage begins—or during the daily speech-making period after legislative business has been disposed of, he will find only a handful of members on the floor and the proceedings dull.

But let our guest drop in at the height of debate, while amendments are being threshed out under the House's five-minute-per-speaker rule when emotions are running high, he'll hear a performance guaranteed to hold his interest. Or for sheer visual enjoyment let him look in upon the Hogarthian scene that unfolds during a quorum or a roll call vote: the floor teeming with members dressed in styles ranging from bland to outlandish, mixing, talking, arm grabbing, huddling secretively, sprawled in their seats, standing and buttonholing each other in the aisles. Here, a cluster milling in the well like a bunch of talkative stevedores at a waterfront shape-up; there, four or five clustered around a storyteller, rearing back in their seats at the punch line with great slapping of thighs and roars of laughter. The buzz of a hundred conversations is so overwhelming that in the days of oral roll calls the Speaker would have to gavel for relative silence so that the reading clerk could hear the members' responses.

And yet minutes after the roll call, the chamber is as quiet as a reading room. The general debate has resumed and the floor is almost empty. At moments like these, if I wanted to escape from the clamor and noise of the press working quarters, I would slip out to the gallery. There I could concentrate with virtually no interruption save the solitary, unexcited voice at the microphone.

Members behave differently on the House floor at night than they do during the day. During the day they are alternately informative, long-winded, occasionally raucous and sometimes nasty. At night they are raucous, nasty and occasionally long-winded and/or informative. This is principally because congressmen do not get paid for overtime and they resent having to hang around the floor until 11 P.M. Knowing that they are going to resent it, they prepare for the experience with dinner and drinks. As a result, you can always count on a nighttime session including the following:

▪ A skonked lawmaker will take the floor and deliver an incoherent, rambling speech which effectively breaks any concentration on the debate that may have been achieved at that point.

▪ Rep. James Haley of Florida will stand up from a seat in the front row, move halfway to the rostrum and the microphone, wave his arms wildly and denounce. Because he doesn't reach the mike, it's never clear whether Haley is denouncing the legislation or those who have forced him to spend his evening in the House. For years I thought that Haley was drunk, but someone who knows him told me once that no, it was just Haley's way of reacting to nocturnal legislating.

▪ Two members will *almost* get into a fist fight. Often one of them is Phil Landrum of Georgia, an amiable enough Georgian at day but supersensitive at night. He usually tangles with other southerners.

▪ About two hours before the debate is supposed to end, a knot of northern Democrats in the far right corner of the chamber will bellow "vote, vote." During the day faceless members of the Pennsylvania delegation are responsible for this chore. At night they are joined by volunteers from other sections of the country.

■ Someone offers a motion to adjourn. That inevitably spurs the Democratic leadership into frenetic activity, for one thing a leader cannot permit is to have the House adjourned from under him. Enough loyalists are still around to save the leadership, and the House stays in session.

For some reason Democratic leaders during the 1960s and 1970s frequently scheduled these inevitably cantankerous nighttime sessions to deal with legislation that would be hard to get through the House during normal hours. This includes the annual foreign aid bills, which would manage to squeak by with a margin of three votes, and measures produced by the old House Un-American Activities Committee (HUAC). The HUAC stuff was not hard to get passed—sponsors could always count on the fear of casting an antipatriotism vote to rope in all except extreme civil libertarians—but it was something else to dispose of the legislation without setting off a brawl.

State of the Union speeches and other momentous addresses have no trouble drawing members of Congress. Most politicians love to tell friends and constituents they were on hand where the action was. They also shoot for the chance of getting on national television. Those two conditions don't apply when the president of Ecuador speaks to a joint session of Congress, so pulling members on to the floor then is a problem for the State Department, congressional leaders and others concerned over the reaction back in Ecuador to the picture of a half-empty chamber. Thus the day before such events the leadership passes the word to members' offices that male staffers would be welcome on the floor tomorrow. Dark suits are suggested.

Should you by chance visit the House during one of those sessions or see a picture of one, take a careful look at the audience. All those intelligent, attentive looking male faces belong to employees. The president of Ecuador won't know but you will.

Eulogizing has always been very big in the House. At the stop of a heartbeat members are on their feet singing paeans to the departed and voicing shock at the news just transmitted to them in a somber and urgent voice by a House member from his home state. This response is likely even if the deceased left the House thirty years before, is unknown to three-quarters of the present membership and slipped peacefully away at the age of ninety-six.

Let it be a *sitting* member who passes away and in addition to the brief, initial reaction a "special order" is arranged at which members take the floor after the close of legislative business one day and speak at some length. Unfortunately, for reasons of scheduling, this sometimes doesn't take place until a few weeks after the death and after most members have overcome their grief and shock. Thus speeches can tend to be longer on words than on sincerity. But it still makes for a touching tribute, with the words inscribed in the *Congressional Record* and bound in a special edition for the family of the departed.

Eulogies are also delivered for retiring members. Often these turn out to be genuine expressions of affection and fun, especially if the member is well-liked and something of a personality. But if the member isn't the type who will inspire the best efforts from the House's champion wits, a visitor walking in on the round of accolades won't be sure whether the subject has retired or died.

Virtues, of course, are found for every honored member. The irascible, bothersome congressman becomes the "energetic advocate of what he believed in." The unheard of, nonachieving individual "worked quietly and effectively on behalf of his constituents, less concerned with publicity than with results." Colleagues who constantly fought with him now speak of the respect they held for him despite their political differences.

Such occasions were guaranteed to be free of the acrimony or contentiousness that could explode at any other time. For Speaker John McCormack they served as therapy. Confronted constantly by Republican challenges, battered from behind by Democratic activists who were dissatisfied with his old-style leadership, McCormack would jump at the opportunity to eulogize someone. He would draw on his vast store of accolades and clichés, gathered over a "last hurrah" lifetime of participation in funerals, graduations and testimonials, throw in personalized remembrances, pay unexcelled tribute to the departed and offer compassionate condolences to the family.

In his Rayburn Building office a congressman looks and feels important. It's much the same when he's at home and attends functions, at almost all of which he is *the* honored guest or one of the dignitaries present. He is singular. But on the floor he is just one of several hundred ordinary-appearing middle-class people, dressed perhaps a little more expensively than the average American but no more distinctively than the hordes who mill about the floor of the New York Stock Exchange. Sitting wherever he can find an empty seat, unsure that anyone in the gallery will recognize him, a representative enjoys far less notice than his counterpart in the Senate, where spectators gawk at the quiet, smaller scene below, searching for the presidential contenders and other celebrities that they have read about. During a quorum call, virtually every visitor will spot Edward Kennedy when he strolls into the Senate. But unless he is pointed out, the casual visitor to the House will almost certainly fail to pick out George Mahon—a congressionally more important member than Kennedy. But House members do not seem to mind the comparative anonymity here. Most seem to truly enjoy the companionship and informality of their legislative club.

Unlike the Senate, the House is not above partaking in old-fashioned Americana. Indeed, it veritably swims in it and boasts of it. Expressions of members' faith-keeping range from an annual foot-tapping musical tribute to Old Glory to thumping endorsements of our commander in chief and his war policies, whoever he may be and whatever they may be.

The first thing the House does every day is to pray, led either by a guest clergyman or by its own chaplain, an official who in 1974 was paid $19,768.80 for the principal duty of delivering a minute of wisdom and inspiration in hopes that the solons would manage to work God's will into their endeavors of statecraft. Unfortunately for them, Him, and us, the House chamber at that moment rarely contains more than half-a-dozen members, including the Speaker, who has to gavel the House into session, the majority and minority leaders, and someone like Rep. H. R. Gross, who is there to make sure they don't auction off the Capitol dome while no one is looking. The rest of the chamber is peopled with pages, clerks and other employees. This attendance record is not quite the shoulder-to-shoulder crowd one expects after having heard House proponents of prayer in public schools denounce the Supreme Court and dare it to try to interfere with *their* daily invocation.

In cooperation with the Senate, the House maintains a

prayer room off the rotunda. An attendant is on duty to prevent tourists from peeking in on meditating members of Congress and to advise about-to-pray lawmakers that the room is occupied. A standing gag around the Capitol is that the prayer room picks up business the closer it gets to election day. The chapel-like facility is not supposed to be used for group services, but in 1965 Rep. Herbert Tenzer of New York brought in a rabbi to conduct High Holiday services for Jewish members. They had found themselves in the Capitol instead of their synagogues after Lyndon Johnson prevailed upon every breathing supporter of self-government for the District of Columbia to be on hand that day and cast a vote for a home rule bill. Their sacrifice and Johnson's herculean effort were not enough to pass the measure, but Speaker McCormack showed his appreciation by donning a yarmulke and paying a visit to the historic service.

To show that they consider religion more than a ritual, about twenty House members meet for breakfast once a week and hear inspirational messages from guest speakers and each other.

Astronauts, America's amalgam of corn and technology, found a home in the House. Although senators were invited to the joint sessions that greeted the first wave of returning spacemen, the representatives were the ones who unabashedly cheered, whistled and provided the enthusiasm for an old-fashioned U.S.A. welcome. During space flights, Science and Astronautics Committee Chairman George Miller would interrupt debates on the floor with breathless and gratifying reports on their progress. But alas, like other Americans, the House eventually lost interest in astronauts. For one trio in 1972 the joint session was replaced by a reception in the Rayburn Building. A handful of law-

makers appeared but, for the most part, the visitors consisted of staff people, and even they weren't in abundance.

Nothing, of course, is more American than the American
flag. Consequently, the House turns it on for Flag Day,
thereby making it one of the few adult gatherings in the
country that still celebrates the June 14 holiday. On the
nearest available free day, usually a Friday, the House puts
on a star-spangled show featuring the pledge of allegiance,
a military color guard, the Joint Chiefs of Staff, and Sousa
marches played by service bands. Delivering the main
address is a prominently patriotic American of the pre-
Pepsi generation, such as Red Skelton or Bob Hope.

As with the daily prayer, the flag draws more adherents
in word than in presence. Members are willing to go a long
way for Old Glory—as they proved during the heated days
of Vietnam War dissent when they tumbled over each other
voting criminal penalties for flag burning—but that doesn't
include spending your day off at the Capitol. Flag Day on
the House floor looks a lot like George Washington's Birthday on the House floor, a day in which a member reads
aloud the Farewell Address. The representatives' chairs are
filled with representatives' kids, pages, staff workers—and a
handful of congressmen.

Except for extraordinary debates, or those held at night
when there is nothing else to do but sit on the floor, most
House members are not in the chamber when amendments
are discussed. Many do hustle over, however, when bells
ring for a vote on an amendment. Unless the proposal was
well advertised, a goodly number of the lawmakers have
little idea of what they are voting for. As they breeze into
the Democratic side of the chamber, Chief Floor Doorman
Warren Jernigan sings out the name of the sponsor. If they

ask, Jernigan will give them a short but surprisingly descriptive and objective explanation of the amendment. Some members can make a judgment right there. If ultra-conservative John Rarick has introduced an amendment to cut funds from an educational bill, liberals will vote "no." Conservatives pouring into the chamber need only to hear that Bella Abzug is the author of an amendment to guarantee a "no" vote on their part. It gets tricky when the name of a middle-of-the-roader is attached to the amendment.

Even though the House has taken a multimillion dollar plunge into the electronics age by turning to the computer for assistance in voting and amassing information, it still records its floor debates and proceedings much the same way as it did one hundred years ago—by hand. An "official reporter" plants him or herself in the midst of a debate and furiously takes down in Gregg shorthand every word uttered. The reporters operate in relays, each transcribing five or six minutes of talk, catching all sides of the debate (which can involve several people, some of them speaking excitedly, unclearly and simultaneously). From the floor the reporters hurry to a room below where they render meaningless what they have just done, undercutting their craftsmanship, by verbally dictating their notes into a recording device from which an expert typist dashes off copies of the exchange.

Within an hour each congressman involved is holding in his hands a transcript of what has been said. If during his time on the floor he had received permission to "revise and extend" his remarks, as most members do, he now has the opportunity to correct faulty grammar, tidy up his delivery and style, substitute temperate words for outcries of rage, and, if he is totally unhappy with what he has said, delete all of his words.

(Congress is the only place where you can wish you hadn't said something and see the wish come true. But this power can occasionally produce mysterious passages in the *Congressional Record*. A member who has had second thoughts about a charge he has just leveled against a colleague will decide to expunge his words. The member he tangled with, however, may not have cooled off yet and wants his retorts left in. Readers of the now one-way exchange will not know who the surviving member was addressing or what he was talking about.)

The approved transcript is then sent to the nearby Government Printing Office (GPO) where it is incorporated into that day's *Congressional Record,* printed that night and delivered the next morning to offices in the Capitol and around town.

It is doubtful whether any more modern system could achieve much faster results than the method the House has been utilizing since the mid-nineteenth century. But one might wonder whether it is the most efficient. Since the reporters are dictating their notes into a dictaphone, why not simply record House sessions and have the typists transcribe the actual words of the members rather than those of the reporters? Not only would cutting out the middleman lead to savings—by eliminating most of the seven-person official reporter staff—but it would minimize the possibility of mistakes and provide an almost indisputable record that could be checked when disputes arise over what a lawmaker said or did not say. Naturally, any such reform talk has been resisted by the reporters, who are exceedingly well paid (nearly $35,000 each in 1974) and are skilled practitioners of a dying art, people who will not wilt under the stress and strain of a demanding job. The seven reporters constitute a unique work force in the House, enjoying a quasi-independent status and the privileges of a medieval guild. They are responsible to no one but the Speaker and comprise the only staff unit in the House that selects its own members. Although now employees of the House, at one time they provided their services on a contract basis, evolving from the pre-*Congressional Record* days before 1873, when a commercial printing firm published a transcript of proceedings, called *The Globe.*

Siding with the reporters are traditionalists among the House membership who would like to see *some* things remain as they have been, lawmakers who believe that the maintenance of certain customs for custom's sake is a noble goal now and then as long as it does not hamper operation of the House, a drawback that cannot be charged to the official reporting system.

The Government Printing Office publishes about 50,000 copies of the *Congressional Record.* It distributes them all over official Washington and mails them to libraries and individuals throughout the world. It is supposed to be the transcript of the previous day's proceedings in Congress, but it is more and less than that. Besides debates and speeches, it incorporates mounds of material that were never spoken on the floor of the House and Senate but were inserted in written form by members. The nonspoken matter also includes such valuable information as a digest of the previous day's events on the floor and in committees, a list of committee meetings scheduled for the day of publication and bills introduced, bills signed by the president, occasional superb and concise summaries of complex issues prepared by members, and periodic reports on the salaries of committee staff aides. (Salaries of personal staffs are published in a separate document.)

The *Record* also includes a lot of garbage. Garbage is defined as the newspaper stories and speeches praising a member, which, because of an overriding sense of modesty on the part of the member, were inserted by a colleague;

poems written by school children; and sixteen reproductions of the same newspaper column that has caught the fancy of sixteen members of Congress.

The *Record* is something less than a transcript of House and Senate sessions because, as has been pointed out, members are permitted to "revise and extend" their remarks. Generally the content is pretty close to the reality, but on occasion it may bear little resemblance to what was actually said. Further diluting the transcript claim of the *Record* is the vast amount of words inserted by members who never participated in a debate but who merely won routine, unanimous consent to include their written pronouncements along with those that were delivered. And finally, the scholars who rely on the *Record* ought also note that even the sequence of speeches is not always accurate. For reasons I have never quite understood, one-minute speeches —those brief statements members make at the start of a session—are sometimes rearranged and stuck in various parts of the *Record*.

All these words cost the taxpayer a fair amount of money. The expense of printing the *Record* in 1975 was estimated at $278 a page. The average *Record* runs nearly 300 pages so that an average per edition cost would be somewhere in the neighborhood of $83,000. A *Record* is published for every day the House or Senate meets, or about four times a week.

For members of Congress who live in the District of Columbia, the GPO will deliver a copy of the *Record* in time for the lawmaker to read with his breakfast. Not everyone appreciates the convenience. William Moorhead of Pittsburgh canceled his home delivery when an issue came crashing through his Georgetown dining room window.

Quaintness has a place in the House. Although solicitors and salesmen are banned from the office buildings and the

Capitol, a special dispensation has been made for The Egg Man. Once a week The Egg Man and his wife drive in from their farm in Winchester, Virginia, and deliver eggs to offices throughout the House. He's been doing it for years, no one quite remembers how he negotiated his monopoly and hardly any of the secretaries and staff aides who patronize him know his real name. He's simply The Egg Man. His customers say his eggs aren't any cheaper than those sold at the supermarkets, but they are fresher.

Around Christmas and Easter, church groups are permitted to come in to sell candles and candy and some enterprising neighborhood black youngsters have been allowed to hawk the *Evening Star* and *News* in the late afternoon. But otherwise the halls of the Cannon, Longworth and Rayburn buildings are free of all salesmen other than those selling expensive office equipment or those seeking congressional help in selling a billion-dollar-weapons system to the Pentagon.

House members like to think of themselves as modest, unpretentious, unswayed by the trappings of power or position and immune to "Potomac fever."

A number of years ago someone pushed to the floor of the House a proposal that would permit each House member to own and display an official House pennant. As one sponsor told his colleagues, boat-owning representatives could sail through coast guard checks and other impediments that ordinary people have to put up with. H. R. Gross and the late Clare Hoffman of Michigan, two truly unpretentious conservatives who enjoyed deflating the pompous, ridiculed the pennant right off the floor with cracks about congressional navies and legislative admirals.

No more was heard about the pennants until 1973. In that year the House stationery store began quietly featuring in its annual catalogue a congressional flag. Made of white cloth, bearing a seal similar to the Presidential Seal, it measures two by three feet and comes with a spindly, unpainted pole. If you order the version with the seal on one side only it costs $11. Two sides will cost you $20. I saw one in a member's office and it reminded me of the flags Boy Scout patrols carried. "It is a little tacky," admitted one defender of the ensign, "but what's wrong with congressmen having their flag? The president, the secretary of state and practically everybody else in government has one."

One of the contentions of this book is that too many members of the House stay too long in the House, that they become too attached, too settled into the place, that in effect they become tenants of the House. Some members, however, have gone even further. They literally live in the House.

Across from the Cannon Office Building is the eight-story House Office Building Annex. It used to be the Congressional Hotel, but a few years ago the House bought it, maintaining it would be needed to meet an increasingly critical shortage of office space. In 1972 the House closed down the hotel, began evicting the lobbyists and others who had offices there, and started converting it to the Annex.

Not evicted was a score of members, including such powerhouses as Wayne Hays, chairman of the House Administration Committee, and Daniel Flood, a senior member of the Appropriations Committee, who had maintained apartments on the hotel's top floor. They stayed on, enjoying a superb location, a full range of services and bargain rents, which now went to the House instead of to the hotel. Before he became GOP Leader, John Rhodes served on the legislative appropriations subcommittee where he unsuccessfully tried to find out how the congressional apartment-dwellers managed to escape eviction, especially in light of the space shortage. He never found out, and when he left the panel in 1974, no one bothered to ask any more.

The unique parliamentary rules under which the House operates serve the House relatively well. Reformers find faults, some of them glaring, with specific parts. But almost everyone familiar with the procedures generally agrees that they do a passable job with a difficult task, which is to permit 435 individuals an adequate opportunity to debate an issue, to do it in a reasonable period of time and with a minimum of confusion. In order to maintain this delicate balance, the House rules are necessarily complex, striving to provide an answer for every eventuality, leaving nothing to chance. Honed and revised over the years, they are the precision tools of a special breed of professional legislators. But to an outsider they can be incomprehensible, filled with gibberish about "moving the previous question," "striking the last word," and "laying on the table."

Unfortunately, sometimes House members forget this. In 1972, as it had for years before, the Republican National Convention functioned under the House rules. The week before the actual convention got underway, the party's Rules Committee gathered at Miami Beach's Eden Roc Hotel to consider some major and controversial changes in the method of selecting delegates. Presiding over the committee as chairman was William Cramer, a former congressman from Florida who looks and sounds like a Jonathan Winters imitation of an unctuous politician.

Determined to keep on schedule, Cramer held his committee tightly to the rules. He rattled off the strange phrases, leaving behind blank looks on the faces of most of the one hundred GOP men and women on the panel. A few House members were on the committee and often they were no better than Cramer. To the laymen in the group it smacked of the show-off—the freshman on his first visit back home, the young soldier on leave after completing basic training, both trying to impress friends by casually dropping into conversation jargon from their new world.

It finally became too much for the noncongressional members of the Rules Committee. One lady stood up and admitted that she didn't know what Cramer and his friends were talking about.

"Why can't we use *Robert's Rules of Order?*" she asked. "Everybody understands that."

Cramer patiently informed the woman that the committee was bound by instructions from the previous convention to operate under House rules. Besides, those rules had served the party well in the past. He clicked on his Jonathan Winters smile, satisfied that he had taken care of the pesky housewife. But before he could get things moving again, a man from the Midwest stood up and said that he agreed with the lady.

"People all over this country know *Robert's*," the man declared. "They use it at PTA meetings, the Kiwanis Club. We all use it in our local Republican organizations. I don't see any reason why we can't use it here. We don't know anything about the House rules and we can't understand them."

His fellow non-House members cheered. Before Cramer and the congressmen knew what had happened, the good Republican men and women had overwhelmingly voted to run the 1976 convention by *Robert's Rules of Order.*

Sometimes even House members don't understand House rules. Whenever the chairman of the Appropriations Committee notifies the House that the panel will be sending a bill to the floor, someone from the minority side of the committee jumps to his feet and exclaims, "Mr. Speaker, I reserve all points of order."

Aside from three or four people, no one in the House knows what this means, including usually the guy who said it. But the ritual has been going on for so long that everybody is embarrassed to ask. Whenever I heard it I would imagine one of the clerks sitting below the Speaker picking up a telephone and dialing a number.

"Hello. Points of Order Room."

"Hi. Speaker's Desk here. Cederberg just reserved a batch for the defense bill."

"Got 'ya."

"Thanks, bye."

Life in Congress a better marriage does not make. Good marriages survive the special rigors—and advantages—that accrue with service in the House or Senate. But few, if any, are bolstered by victory on election day. Publicly, politicians are forever crediting "the woman behind the man" with providing the brains and spirit that led to his success. More often than not the little woman is behind the man all right, gritting her teeth and enduring a trying ordeal.

Congressmen shuttle between Washington and their districts, some spending almost every weekend back home, others lucky, indifferent or far enough away so that they can get by with one or two weekends a month. A wife is left with the choice of moving to the Washington area, where she can see her husband during the week and do without him on the weekends, or stay at home and share him on weekends with his political commitments. Obviously, she's likely to see more of her mate if she moves to Washington, but this can be difficult for a family whose children are well along in school and for a wife who has to uproot herself from a career or strong community ties.

Adding to the problem is the unique environment the congressman circulates in during his work day. At the Capitol he comes into daily contact with an inordinate number of young, single, impressionable and attractive women. Some of them develop nothing more threatening than unexpressed adoration for their bosses. Still others, though, proffer a wide range of possible relationships, from the frivolous to the serious, neither of which strengthens the congressman's marriage.

Should our member's union already be undergoing a strain, the Capitol Hill atmosphere could supply the *coup de grace*. Rather than squarely face the problems and try to resolve them, he is likely to run away from the bickering at home and retreat to his Camelot where he is surrounded by people who instantly and cheerfully do his bidding, eager to extend respect and sometimes affection.

Many marriages end in divorce, or separation, and an indeterminate number remain intact on the surface but in reality have withered away to little more than an arrangement or understanding in which both partners agree to maintain a façade. Statistics aren't available to prove or disprove it, but my suspicion is that the marriage breakup rate among members of Congress is higher than the national average for couples of similar social, economic and educational backgrounds.

Michigan representatives have been particularly hard hit. Six of the nineteen-member delegation to the Ninety-second Congress (1971 and 1972) broke up with their wives during that two-year period. It was strictly a bipartisan disaster—three Republicans and three Democrats. And, according to one observer of Michigan politics, "the delegation is less playboyish than most around here. It doesn't have the reputation that, say, some of the Californians have. None of the six Michigan guys really had a reputation for playing around."

One Michigan marriage that did survive was that of Gerald and Betty Ford, even though the demands on his time, as GOP Leader in the House, were far greater than on any of his colleagues. His elevation to the presidency may actually have relieved some of the pressure. Once he was chosen House Republican Leader in 1965, Ford embarked on a nationwide crusade to elect Republicans to the House. He criss-crossed the country, speaking at fundraisers and any other party functions that would aid in the effort. When he wasn't on the road, he obligingly showed up at the endless number of semiofficial affairs in Washington to which the House GOP Leader is invited. By 1973 he figured he averaged four out of seven nights a week away from home. In some ways Betty Ford and the couple's four children paid a higher price than he did, sharing as they did in the disruptive effects of his work but deriving none of the immediate satisfaction that he gained from it. Shortly before leaving the House, Ford frankly acknowledged it hadn't been easy.

"It doesn't adversely affect me as much as it affects my wife. She has grown to be sort of very unhappy about it. I think my children have understood quite well although I think they object to a growing degree now. I think the net result is that most of our children would not like to be in politics."

3

"I Never Get Caught in the Rain"

IT IS A JULY morning in Washington. The heat and humidity are already uncomfortably high. Air pollution is beginning to climb to threatening levels with the first wave of rush hour traffic. But inside our congressman's contemporary and expensive home the air is cool and clear. The house is in McLean, Virginia. It could just as easily be in Bethesda, Maryland, or northwest Washington.

He combines breakfast with a quick reading of the *Washington Post*. And even if its liberalism should infuriate him, he grudgingly concedes that it is an awfully readable paper, preparing him as it does for the topics of the day's floor speeches and cloakroom conversation as well as filling him in on Washington gossip.

After breakfast our congressman slips from the kitchen to his attached garage, momentarily gasping one of the few breaths of fresh air he will breathe that day, climbs into a late model, high-priced, air-conditioned car and drives to work. The route he takes is revealing in what it does not reveal. First through McLean, with its $75,000-and-above

38

homes and its quaint village shopping area. Then on to the George Washington Memorial Parkway, a lovely federally built and maintained road along the Potomac River. Our motorist skims through the woods, ascends the palisades above the Potomac, catching a glimpse through the trees of the rapids far below. He leaves the parkway at the Memorial Bridge, a concrete span of settled dignity symbolically intended to reunite North and South, and is met at the District of Columbia side by the nation's monuments to Lincoln, Jefferson and Washington. Unlike such cities as New York and Los Angeles, where tightly packed traffic either spins along at harrowing speeds or bumps ahead with frustrating stops and starts, the traffic here seems to glide at a comfortable pace, giving drivers time for an occasional and safe glance at the Tidal Basin. Shortly before he reaches Independence Avenue and the city streets, our congressman veers off to the right and ascends the Southwest Freeway. Typical of elevated highways throughout the country, this one was built during the 1960s and seems especially designed for members of the House.

It swings them around, up and over the urban ugliness they were elected to worry about and, if possible, do something about. As it is, most of them find it difficult to remember that it is even there.

In less than three minutes our lawmaker has circled the choked streets of downtown Washington and is exiting at the very foot of the Rayburn Building. There, a Capitol policeman stops opposite-bound traffic, waves him into the building's garage and passes him on to a parking attendant who greets him with a cheerful "Good morning, Congressman."

There are enough garage levels, parking spaces and elevators in the Rayburn Building so that every one of its 169 congressional occupants can park his car within a few steps from an elevator near his office. (Although the Capitol physician, following a rash of heart attacks among his patients a few years ago, has been advising congressmen to get daily exercise, the House so abounds in conveniences that unless the lawmaker makes it down to the gym for a regular workout he is hard pressed to follow the doctor's advice.)

Breezing into his office he is met by good mornings from secretaries and aides. The receptionist hands him the phone messages that have already started flowing in, his administrative assistant follows him inside into his private office and briefs him on the day's first and most important problems. The ice and the *Congressional Record* have been delivered, the coffee is perking, the opened mail lies on his desk. He fires out orders to get so-and-so, to find out about such-and-such a meeting. It's a Hollywood portrayal of the important executive.

Throughout the day every step is preceded by servantry. So that he doesn't have to wait along with everyone else, each bank of elevators contains one reserved for "members only." (It is run by an operator—even though it is automatic. Administration Committee Chairman Wayne Hays decreed the special arrangement in 1973 on grounds that members needed all the help they could get in making the new, speeded-up electronic roll calls. What Hays does not explain is why they are also reserved on days and at times when the House is not in session.)

Seats are reserved for him on the subway between the Rayburn Building and the Capitol. If his office is in the Longworth or Cannon buildings and he chooses to go outside for the walk to the Capitol rather than traverse the connecting tunnel, police will regulate the traffic signal at the intersection of Independence and New Jersey avenues in order that he not be delayed by a lengthy red light. (Rep.

Clarence Long of Maryland grew so accustomed to the service that he began anticipating it. He would often plunge across the busy corner with or without the light, seemingly convinced that he had been elected to immortality as well as to a seat in Congress. The alarmed cop on the intersection would fling himself into the street, frantically bringing cars to a screeching halt as the determined Long hurried across, oblivious to the commotion.)

Around and on the House floor a retinue of aides, parliamentarians, pages, attendants, doormen and assorted hangers-on advise, provide and adulate. In the immediate vicinity of the floor our member can nap in his party's cloakroom, read his hometown newspaper in the Speaker's lobby, bolt down a quick sandwich in the snack bar, grab a shine in the men's room and secure a precedent from the parliamentarian's office for an upcoming legislative battle.

Camaraderie abounds. Back slapping. Joshing. Stories. Decent guys. Not all of them his type, but enough solid friends to make a man feel good.

A lunchtime visit to the members' dining room vividly reinforces—if any reinforcement is necessary—the private club atmosphere that pervades the House. Jovial headwaiter Ernest Pettinaud greets our member by name; Negro waiters in white coats serve him in antebellum style, and he ends the meal by signing for the check. Guests are impressed, and if privacy is desired smaller rooms are scattered about the Capitol and the Rayburn Building for group luncheons.

And so it goes through the day, a day ended perhaps on a note of relaxation—drinks with colleagues, either at a hideaway in the Capitol or at one of the social clubs the two parties run on the Hill. Or maybe he will crack open a bottle in the office and put one down with the staff.

The ride home is pleasant. The monuments, now softly

bathed in floodlights, help with the unwinding. Out of sight as they were in the morning, are the decaying row houses, the tattered garden apartments which constitute much of Washington's public housing, the ragtag kids on the streets, the broken men on the corner. In 1968 the smoke rose high over the black slum and it frightened him. But tonight the sky is clear and family and dinner are waiting.

An observant House member, looking back on his ten years in Washington, remarked to a friend one day in 1973 that life indeed was good for congressmen.

"You know, I never get caught in the rain. Literally, I never get wet. When you think about it, it's incredible. I drive to work and park in a garage under my office. I take a subway from the Rayburn Building to the Capitol. When I go to the airport someone drives me right to the front entrance. And when I land there's someone to pick me up. It's like that all the time."

He paused, reflecting on what he had just said. It was apparent he had never viewed his circumstances in quite that light. It was having an impact.

"It's incredible," he repeated. "I never get caught in the rain."

Our congressman differs from most of his 434 colleagues only in his degree of perceptiveness and his willingness to admit that government-provided creature comforts do much to ease the hard work and strain that accompany congressional service. What he might have added is that the House took a quantum jump toward the good life at an historically embarrassing time, the mid- and late-1960s.

When racial tensions were literally erupting into fiery and frightening confrontations, when Americans and Asians were killing each other by the thousands and when their constituents were worried sick over one or both events, members of the House of Representatives were hiking their pay by 80 percent; increasing their number of free round trips home by 1,700 percent; augmenting the House work force by about a third; completing and occupying one of the most expensively inefficient buildings in the history of western civilization and improving their pension plan to the point where a member with thirty years experience could retire at three times the amount of money that he was earning when he first came to Congress.

The House had put the war years to businesslike use. By 1974, members enjoyed an array of taxpayer-provided emoluments that would have shamed the most beneficent of socialist governments. Among the highlights of The Good Life on the Hill:

■ *Pay*—In 1963, when the presence of American advisors constituted the extent of U.S. military involvement in Vietnam, members of Congress were receiving an annual salary of $22,500. Ten years later, when the last American bomber touched down in Thailand and brought an end to American fighting in Indochina, the lawmakers were pulling in $42,500 and pressing for an immediate boost of $10,000 plus. They failed because the Senate decided it was inappropriate for Congress to be raising its pay while many in the country were reeling from the staggering blows of inflation.

■ *Pensions*—Unlike millions of Americans who after working long and hard years must live out their days on a standard just over or below the poverty level, life for the politically successful congressman need not sour at retirement. With the member and the government each contributing 8 percent of his salary, lawmakers qualify for a pension based on the three highest paid years of federal service (including up to five years of military duty). It ranges from 12.5 percent of salary after five years to 80 percent after thirty-two years. A member who retired in 1974 after thirty years of combined military and congressional service would net an annual pension of $31,875. At the time he took office he earned $10,000 a year. Presently, the maximum pension a member can draw is $34,000 after thirty-two years.

■ *Life Insurance and Death Gratuities*—As soon as he takes office a lawmaker automatically qualifies for a $45,000 life insurance policy—regardless of his health or age. In 1974 it cost him or her $26.82 a month. In addition, should a member die in office a widow or other survivor is almost automatically voted a death gratuity of one year's salary, which at the moment means another $42,500.

■ *Health Insurance and Medical Care*—Besides being eligible for the Federal Employees Health Benefits Program, which is similar in premiums and coverage to most group health plans, members may avail themselves of free and convenient preventive and emergency medical care through the Capitol Physician's Office, a fully equipped clinic located in the basement of the Capitol and staffed by navy doctors, nurses and corpsmen. Members there can undergo a complete physical examination, receive therapy treatment for aches and pains as well as obtain complete X ray, laboratory and drug services. Because of the age of most of his patients, and the stress they might encounter, the Capitol physician has been pushing a program to avert heart attacks. It includes submitting members to regular electrocardiograms (and furnishing them with a wallet-size copy of the test), stocking resuscitation equipment in the Speaker's lobby just off the House floor, training doorkeepers and other staff aides in emergency treatment of heart attack victims, and keeping a navy ambulance parked behind the Capitol. The navy physicians working in the clinic are at most minutes away from a member (or anyone else) stricken at the Capitol. Finally, members of Congress are welcome at the Walter Reed Army Hospital and Bethesda Naval Hospital, where they can receive excellent medical care in VIP quarters at rates considerably below those charged at civilian hospitals in the area. (In 1974 a member of Congress was charged $133 a day. The bill covered the costs of a private room, physician fees and medicine.)

■ *Taxes*—A little noticed section of the Internal Revenue Code permits congressmen to deduct up to $3,000 a year to cover the expenses of living away from their official residence, the one back in the district. Because Congress now meets for most of the year, the provision amounts virtually to a $3,000 standard deduction.

■ *Cash Allowances*—Certain official allowances can be translated into direct cash payments. One is for stationery. Each member is provided with $6,500 a year for the purchase of office supplies. He can keep the money on account at the House stationery store, where he is able to purchase a wide range of office supplies—as well as such items as wallets and fountain pens that are suitable for personal use and gifts—at cut rates. Or he can take the cash and buy his supplies on the commercial market. In either event, he may pocket whatever is left over. Before 1974, when the allowance was $4,250, many members, especially those activists who regularly churned out press releases, published lengthy reports and sent out a lot of mass mailings, complained that the $4,250 wasn't enough to cover their stationery expenses and that they were forced to dip into their personal or political campaign funds to cover the deficit. But others, especially the low profile, moribund, safe-district members managed to turn a tidy profit. For example, when Rep. Watkins Abbitt, a Virginia Democrat, retired in 1972 he took with him $21,900 he had accumulated from the stationery account over a period of twenty-four years in the House.

Members may also retain for their personal use unspent travel allowances, money intended to cover the costs of journeying between constituents at home and the business of government in Washington. They have the option of accepting reimbursement (at the rate of twelve cents a mile plus 10 percent) for a maximum of thirty-six round trips during every two-year Congress, or taking a lump sum of $4,500. The choice produces some strange results. In 1973 four congressmen from the Maryland and Virginia suburbs of Washington claimed their full $2,250 per year allowance. In dollars and cents this translated into a commuting subsidy, something not available to their colleagues, staff members or anyone else in Congress who has to commute to the Capitol every day. The four were Republicans, all of whom like to think of themselves as fiscal conservatives and protectors of the taxpayers' money. Interestingly, Rep. Gilbert Gude, considered a bit too liberal and free spending for most of his fellow Republicans, has never claimed any travel allowances for his daily drive from suburban Montgomery County, Maryland. Nor has the District of Columbia's delegate, Walter Fauntroy, even though he too is eligible.

■ *Junketing*—Another form of subsidized travel, the overseas version, is available to members and, sometimes, to their wives as well. Virtually any member who wants to, can arrange to fly to Europe or the Far East or almost anywhere else for a VIP tour of such cities as Paris, Rome, London, Tokyo and Hong Kong. The costs ranges from zero for himself to budget rates for his wife. Technically the sojourns constitute "official travel," and are "study missions" or "inspection trips" designed to gather information for

Congress on U.S. activities and interests abroad. Often the trips indeed offer this potential, affording serious lawmakers an excellent opportunity, for example, to assess a particular foreign aid program rather than relying on an official Washington evaluation from the Agency for International Development. In the same vein, a congressman can develop an understanding and a feel for foreign policy issues that can be achieved only through firsthand experience. But realistically speaking, many representatives look upon the opportunity as a vacation, one that includes free transportation for him and his wife aboard an air force jet, a $75-a-day expense account, receptions, cocktail parties and dinners in honor of him and his colleagues, and constant attention by the local U.S. embassy staff and the host government. While the lawmakers attend the few working sessions scheduled, wives are taken on sightseeing and shopping tours of the city. Most congressmen limit themselves to one overseas junket a year, and a fair number of homebodies never leave the United States. But some avid globetrotters squeeze in two or three a year, catching Europe on one jaunt, the Far East on another and perhaps Latin America on a third. Generally avoided by this bunch are the world's underdeveloped countries, with their depressing scenes of malnutrition, poverty and teeming slums. Those are left for staff investigators and a handful of concerned members.

  ■ *Recreation*—Unlike the International Monetary Fund, the House does not run a country club on the outskirts of Washington for the relaxation and enjoyment of its members. But it does have a gym in the Rayburn Building in which members can play paddle ball, exercise, take a swim, and get a massage. Women members have their own room with limited "health facilities" and at specified times may use the pool in the men's gym.

■ *Hideaways*—Not included on any official list of emoluments are the small rooms scattered about the Capitol and doled out to the most senior lawmakers. Approximately seventy-five such rooms, according to *Congressional Quarterly,* are located on the House and Senate sides. Occupants are able to slip away from the floor to get some work done or rest without having to trek long distances back to their regular offices. They also serve as convenient watering holes for a friendly drink. Some skeptics call them "nooky rooms," suspecting that they serve as hideaways for daytime trysts. But that appellation appears to have originated in an earlier era, when the average age of senior members was much younger. For the present tenants, most of whom are in their sixties, seventies and eighties, the issue is largely academic. Whatever their use, critics contend the hideaways are a waste of a precious commodity, noting that for years House leaders have argued for extension of the Capitol on grounds that there is a critical shortage of space.

■ *Self-perpetuity*—Of all the benefits coming his way, the most important is the one a member realizes simply by being a member. At election time, the odds favor the incumbent over the challenger, and they get better each time around. A study conducted by the Library of Congress covering the eight elections between 1956 and 1972 showed that an average of 93 percent of the incumbents won in the general election. The percentages ranged from a low of 88.4 in 1964 to a high of 98.8 in 1968. And aside from years in which major redistricting took place—when incumbents would be forced to run against each other—no more than seven members were ever knocked off in primaries.

Besides the access an office-holder commands to the media, and the contact he is able to maintain with voters by servicing their requests, the incumbent is also able to campaign for reelection at government expense. He can assign his government-paid staff aides to campaign chores. He can walk down to the government-subsidized recording studio in the basement of the Rayburn Building and at reduced cost, with the aid of free professional advice, cut a polished tape of his weekly television report to constituents. Or he can do a one-minute phone beeper for local radio stations. And although his free postage privilege is supposed to be limited to nonpolitical mail, it's pretty hard to imagine a more politically effective ploy than shortly before election day to send thousands of "postal patrons" his newsletter or reprints of a speech that he placed in the *Congressional Record.*

Amazingly, many members of Congress attacked as outrageous and revolutionary—and knocked out of the 1974 campaign reform bill—a proposal to finance all federal election campaigns with public funds. What really upset them was the possibility that their challengers would begin to receive a portion of the subsidies they have been reaping all along.

The benefits list goes on. Some can be termed incidentals. Others are not so incidental. Representatives enjoy plants furnished by the botanic garden, meals cheaper than they would pay in a nongovernment subsidized restaurant, free parking under their offices, $2 haircuts (which while considerably cheaper than the commercial version is still $2 more than senators pay at their barber shop), reduced rates at some Washington hotels, an opportunity to get their kids summer jobs in the House running elevators or raking leaves, a congressionally drawn taxi zone system that permits them and anyone else on Capitol Hill to reach most downtown offices for less than a dollar and unlimited sick leave during each Congress. This last benefit has led on occasion to a situation in which a congressman ailing at the start of the first session collects pay for virtually his entire two-year term without having once voted. And then there are the vacations.

About the first action that leaders take after a new Congress convenes, is to issue a schedule of breaks for the session. Before the first major piece of legislation has cleared the floor, the House has put one or two hefty recesses under its belt. In 1970 the House and Senate officially established a summer recess, a move which provided UPI's Dick West, who writes a daily humor column from Capitol Hill, with a ready answer for those friends who ask him what Congress has been doing:

> "Congress is building up," I reply.
> "Building up to what?"
> "Building up to their summer vacation," I explain.
> For the first time, this year, you see, Congress has scheduled a summer recess. It was adopted as part of the congressional reform program advocated by a group of the younger lawmakers.
> In fact, it was the only part of the reform that was adopted.
> The reformers argued that Congress could function more efficiently if they had a regular summer vacation, with the dates fixed in advance rather than having to improvise time off while the session was in progress.
> So the dates were fixed last winter—August 13 to September 3.
> Well, you could hardly expect Congress to plunge into a summer recess for the first time without any training or practice. Ergo, much of this year's session has been devoted to getting into condition for the recess.
> Members have been building up to it gradually, which was a wise approach. Otherwise, some of them might have been over-extended.
> They began tuning up with the Lincoln Day recess (February 7–17), took a trial run at Eastertime (April 3–

14) and rehearsed again over Memorial Day (May 28–
June 2).

The legislative program was kept to a minimum during
the weeks preceding and following each of these warm-up
recesses, and a number of long weekends were interspersed
between them.

The House, for instance, held its Flag Day ceremony two
days early this week, making it unnecessary to meet on
Saturday.

The last recess before the big one will be Independence
Day (July 2–7). By the time the lawmakers finish it, they
should be in peak condition and ready to go the distance
in August.

For years a boost in benefits was relatively hard to come
by, for the simple reason that the House, in open session,
had to pass a bill or resolution to raise its take from the
Treasury. Various ploys were utilized in efforts to slide
something by the press and such economy watchdogs as
Republicans H. R. Gross and Durward Hall, two men who
made a habit of blowing the whistle on their fellows whenever they felt it was deserved. Archaic terms and formulas
were retained for their obscurity potential. Authorizing
members to expand the size of their personal staffs was
called an increase in "clerk hire." Staff salaries were pred-
icated on "base pay," a salary level that had been established decades before. Pay hikes would be added to that
figure but it took a fair amount of digging through the
records to finally figure out that the employee listed on the
public record as making $4,000 was actually making
$10,400. That gambit got so confusing that even congress-
men began to lose track of how much their aides were
pulling in. So in the mid-1960s the House started issuing

payrolls like everybody else, listing a $10,400-a-year secretary as earning $10,400.

Another technique practiced by the dispensers of largess was to send in Sam Friedel, chairman of the House Administration Committee during the late 1960s. Armed with a bill or resolution drawn by his gift-giving committee, Friedel would submerge his native Baltimore accent into a gravelly-voiced garble and offer an explanation that was incomprehensible. It was like listening to the old double-talk comedian, Al Kelly.

In one such performance, Friedel was mumbling his way through an Administration Committee bill that was complex when described in clear English. Gross asked Friedel to explain a point. Friedel stared hopelessly across the chamber at his questioner, paused, then answered: "I will only say to the gentleman that the legislation speaks for itself." One suspected but could never prove that Friedel was as good a showman as Kelly.

Nevertheless, there were even limits to what Friedel could slip through the House. Besides the hollering of Gross and Hall, my boss, UPI's Frank Eleazer, kept a lonely journalistic lookout for boondoggles the Administration Committee helped to quietly whisk through the House. If possible, Eleazer found out ahead of time what was in the works and often spiked it by writing an advance story.

In 1971 the Democratic powers came up with an ingenious scheme to guarantee a continuous flow of emoluments with a minimum of embarrassment. The House Administration Committee, under its strong, new chairman, Wayne Hays, drafted a resolution which authorized the committee, on its own, to furnish members with added and new benefits. No House debate or vote was required; no public announcement was needed.

On July 21, 1971, with most Republicans objecting, the

House passed the resolution on a 233 to 167 roll call vote. Invested with its new authority, the Administration Committee wasted little time making up for missed past opportunities. Members profited. Whether taxpayers did is arguable. During the July 21 debate, Rep. Frank Thompson, a prominent House liberal and a senior member of the Administration Committee, assured his colleagues that the resolution was designed simply to spare the House the time-consuming and absurd task of considering "every bit of minutia with respect to the routine daily operations of this side of Congress."

The Administration Committee plunged right into its minutia-relieving chore. Within two weeks it handed down "Committee Order No. 1," an edict which upped from one to three the number of offices a congressman could maintain in his district at government expense. Before the year was out the committee reached the logical conclusion that with all those offices to take care of members would have to get home more often. Thus, "Committee Order No. 2" boosted the number of free round trips home from one during each month the House was in session to twenty-four for the entire two-year term, a net gain of two or three. Less than a year later Order No. 2 was revised and members were informed that the maximum number of trips had been raised to thirty-six, or for those who preferred the lump sum payment, from $1,500 to $2,250 per Congress.

By mid-1974, the Administration Committee had issued fourteen orders. The net cost to the taxpayers totaled about $16 million annually. The sum was not staggering by government standards. Nor can we say that the increase in stationery allowance, the extra trips home and the added district offices were not justified. But there was no House debate, the Administration Committee held no hearings on the proposals, no warning was given that they were even being considered and no publicity accompanied their adoption.

In the style of a monarch, Chairman Hays would issue the royal proclamations from his out-of-the-way but lavishly furnished turret under the Capitol dome. Since the order invariably made life better for the recipient, few objected to it and those that might, such as H. R. Gross, couldn't do anything about it if they wanted to.

In effect, the House had empowered fourteen individuals (a bare majority of the Administration Committee) to conduct unfettered raids on the Treasury. No action by the House or the Senate, nor any approval by the president was necessary. True, the money still had to be included in an appropriation that had to be formally enacted into law. But in actuality this check was almost meaningless. By the time the legislative appropriation bill was being considered, the Administration Committee had already issued its "order," members had already hired the new aides and spent the extra allowances or at least made commitments to do so.

Elected officials of the government were enriching their positions without restraint from any other branch, out of public view and in a manner that enabled almost all members to escape responsibility for any public voter indignation that might arise.

🚩

Like nothing else possibly could, the Rayburn Office Building demonstrates the self-indulgent and bureaucratic leanings of the House. The Rayburn Building is aesthetically gross, outrageously expensive and absurdly impractical. It is also illegal. In a way it is a lot like the war in Vietnam, for which the House was only partly responsible.

Much has been written about the looks and cost of the structure; little has been written about its unsavory origins. The story is worth telling, if for no other reason than it might help explain the travesties that followed.

The Rayburn Building was born on March 18, 1955. In a legislative sense, it might be said that the birth was premature. Speaker Sam Rayburn employed his considerable skills, enormous prestige and powerful influence to slip the project through the House and by an unsuspecting public. Rayburn died in 1961; before the building was finished his colleagues decided to name it after him. It was Rayburn's seventeen-year record as Speaker and not his performance that afternoon in March, 1955, which won him the honor. But he deserved it on either count.

At Rayburn's urging the Appropriations Committee had included in a supplemental appropriation the not unreasonable provision that $25,000 was to be spent studying ways to meet an obvious and increasingly serious shortage of office space. But once the bill got to the floor Rayburn, departing from his usual role, offered an amendment that would up the $25,000 to "$2 million and such additional sums as may be necessary." And instead of spending the money to study the problem, the funds would be used to acquire a site and to immediately start construction. In other words, the House would be off and running toward erection of a third office building.

Rayburn was proposing virtually blank check financing of it, even though the structure had not yet been designed and no one, with the possible exception of Rayburn, had any idea of how much it would all cost. The procedure was not only illogical, it also violated House rules. Before the House can appropriate money, Congress must have passed a separate "authorization" measure. In this case, Congress had enacted an authorization for a study but none for full-scale construction. Theoretically, any member could block the Rayburn amendment simply by raising a point of order.

Rep. Clare Hoffman, an irascible Republican from Michigan who looked sternly and skeptically at the spending of public moneys for any purpose, jumped to his feet.

"Point of order, Mr. Chairman," he bellowed.

Nothing happened. In the chair was Rep. Clark Thompson, Rayburn's fellow Texan, or, in the words of H. R. Gross, Hoffman's longtime friend and ally, Rayburn's "stooge." Hoffman renewed his call. Still no response. The proceedings moved on. Finally Hoffman gained recognition and made the point of order. Thompson ruled it came too late.

In exasperation, Hoffman shouted that he had been on his feet seeking recognition even before the reading clerk had finished reading the Rayburn amendment.

"That," Thompson replied blandly, "was not the proper time."

The only possible obstacle was out of the way. Appropriations Committee Chairman Clarence Cannon, normally a venerable advocate of economy in government, spoke of the space "emergency" faced by the House and asked members to approve their Speaker's amendment. To no one's surprise, it breezed through and the Rayburn Building was on its way.

Eleven times between 1955 and 1964 the House voted funds for the project. In 1957 Gross tried to block a $7.5 million installment, but by then progress had reached the point where enough had gone into the building so that proponents could use the argument favored by sponsors of ballooning weapon systems: if we quit now we'll be wasting all we've spent so far. Gross lost 206 to 176.

What the congressmen, and the taxpayers, got for their money was fifty-four acres of marble, granite, limestone and terrazzo, shaped into a mammoth classic design of indeterminate period. Inside its nine stories (half of which are below ground) were three-room office suites for 169 representatives, a 1600-car garage, 9 two-story high committee hearing rooms, 16 subcommittee rooms, staff rooms, anterooms, conference rooms, storage rooms, press rooms, maintenance rooms, a cafeteria, a carryout shop, a barber shop and all the other facilities necessary to support the 2,800 people planners figured would be working in the building, and the uncountable number of visitors.

In one support function, the Rayburn Building stands unexcelled. It contains more rest rooms per occupant than probably any similar structure in the history of modern civilization. Interestingly, a severe bathroom shortage exists in the Capitol, so serious that on the House side there are only two ladies' rooms with a grand total of four commodes, to serve the thousands of women and children who troop through each day. But the visitors find quick relief if they can make it over to the Rayburn Building, where House leaders compensated with a vengeance for the scarcity in the Capitol. Rest rooms, for both sexes and of every size, abound, all appointed with handsome and expensive marble and chrome fixtures. Public rest rooms alone number ninety. Every office, of course, includes a private lavatory for the congressman and originally one was provided for the staff, although some staff facilities have since been ripped out to provide more working space. The staffs of committees and subcommittees are similarly taken care of and still more rest rooms are scattered throughout the building for maintenance and service workers. House officials claim not to have any idea how many rest rooms are in the Rayburn Building but some simple addition, multiplication and extrapolation produces a conservative estimate of 440, including 600 commodes and 650 sinks.

As silly as accounting of bathrooms might seem, it points up one of the unique qualities of the Rayburn Building—its towering impracticality. Unless an army occupied the place, there's no way to justify 400 bathrooms. Shortly before it opened in 1965, *Chicago Daily News* reporters James McCartney and Charles Nicodemus compared the Rayburn Building, in terms of cost and space available, to two other large office buildings, the Merchandise Mart in Chicago and the Empire State Building on Manhattan island. To the surprise of Rayburn critics, they disclosed that the $81.3 million cost of the building was in line with the cost of the other two structures, taking into account inflation. But they also discovered, as the following table indicates, that for $81.3 million the House of Representatives was getting far less for its money than the owners of the Merchandise Mart and the Empire State Building.

Building	Usable/Rental space	Number of workers
Rayburn	935,000 sq. ft.	2,800
Merchandise Mart	3,300,000 sq. ft.	25,000
Empire State	2,158,000 sq. ft.	20,000

Eating up much of the space, of course, is the three-level garage. Nevertheless, there are vast stretches of emptiness, both horizontally and vertically, that serve no utilitarian purpose and contribute little beauty to an edifice that is sorely in need of both. On Independence Avenue a wide balcony extends two full blocks along the side of the building. There is no earthly reason why anyone would want to walk the steps leading right and left from the entrance up to the balcony. It doesn't go anywhere and its design offers nothing more inviting to strollers than a vast expanse of granite. In eight years I can't recall seeing anyone on it.

The committee hearing rooms are of good size—vertically. They stand two stories high. Unfortunately, they are not very deep; so shallow, in fact, that only 130 seats are provided for the waiting witnesses, the contingent of backup experts who accompany testifying officials and spectators. The absurdity of the design was pointedly underscored in May, 1974, when the Judiciary Committee began open hearings into the impeachment of President Nixon. After the scores of reporters and the special guests were seated there was virtually no room for ordinary citizens to view the historic event.

Occupying more space are the gym facilities—several slumber rooms, a 20-by-60-foot pool, a steam room and paddle ball courts. Although one end of the pool is a good ten feet deep, there is no diving board. For good reason. The ceiling here, as opposed to those in committee rooms, is so low, noted McCartney and Nicodemus that "any congressman taking the slightest bounce would doubtless crack his cranium on the plaster above."

Aesthetically, the Rayburn Building has not fared well with the critics. *The New York Times*'s Ada Louise Huxtable wrote of it on March 30, 1965:

"Architecturally the Rayburn Building is a national disaster. Its defects range from profligate mishandling of fifty acres of space to elephantine esthetic banality at record costs. . . . It is quite possible that this is the worst building for the most money in the history of the construction art. It stuns by sheer mass and boring bulk."

But Rep. Tom Steed, a past chairman of the legislative appropriations subcommittee, told his colleagues in that same month that they needn't be ashamed of how the building looked or how much it cost.

"It is designed to stand with time," Steed declared, "and no one need apologize if it has grandeur and majesty—that is what it ought to have."

So in February, 1965, the same month that Lyndon Johnson ordered American bombers over North Vietnam in Operation Rolling Thunder, the House of Representatives moved into its palace above the old Tiber Creek sewer.

The tale of the Rayburn Building closes on a note of irony. Approximately $100 million was spent acquiring land, constructing the building, furnishing it and linking it to the Capitol with a twenty-five-second subway ride. Yet in spite of all this money, in spite of the determination to achieve a "grandeur and majesty" that could not be matched by the Senate or the other two branches of government, the House is still short on office space, the condition which led to putting up the Rayburn Building in the first place.

In many of the members' three-room suites the staff is so crammed together that the representative's own office has to be called into service, assuming the member is egalitarian enough to tolerate what some of his colleagues would consider an indignity. Summer interns, perhaps a massive piece of office equipment, or maybe both, might be installed there. Considering the spacious office and reception area that an obscure agency official and his secretary command, the Rayburn Building residents might well wonder who calls the shots in Washington.

One reason for the overcrowding is the enormous waste of space. The building is awash in alcoves, nooks and recesses that serve no function but are a result of the building's design. Part of the wastage is unavoidable but some of it clearly results from pointless opulence. Hearings could be just as productive in a one-story committee hearing room as they are in two story rooms. Corridors would be just as useful if their width permitted only one instead of two cars to pass through them.

A second, more interesting reason for the overcrowding is the failure of Rayburn and the other senior members who planned the building to come anywhere near anticipating the expansion that would take place in members' staffs. When the House voted its first appropriation for the building in 1955, members were authorized a maximum of ten employees. By 1973 the figure had climbed to sixteen. Little provision was made for growth. The size of the Rayburn Building suites was literally locked in cement, each bounded by permanent walls.

Either Rayburn and his cronies goofed monumentally in not foreseeing the growth trend or else they were satisfied that ten assistants were plenty for any congressman.

And finally, despite all the money spent on the building, it didn't occur to any of its planners to spend some of it for air conditioning of the kitchen in the cafeteria. It wasn't until 1974, after recently appointed Capitol Architect George White described the summer working conditions there as unbearable, that the House provided funds to install air conditioning for the employees there.

In the 1960s members of the House of Representatives came into what could be called The Good Life. For some it was no more and often less than they would have enjoyed had they remained private citizens. But those were either the wealthy, or men whose careers had been or would have been marked by corporate elegance far surpassing anything government could match. To the mildly competent lawyers, the fairly successful businessmen, the ex-teachers, union leaders, athletes and longtime local politicians, membership in the House, complete with all the perquisites and trappings of the office, represented the capstone of a lifetime.

Those trappings and perquisites also provided a reason —other than devotion to public service—why some members remain in the House so long.

4

Whose House?

BACK IN 1789, representatives were about all there was to the House of Representatives. Sixty-five "very good" but not "shining men," as Fisher Ames, a member of that first Congress put it, gathered together in New York City and racked up a record of accomplishment that has not been surpassed since.

Without tradition, staff or lobbyists to guide them, they set up the departments and agencies of the new government, established a judiciary, passed more than sixty major pieces of legislation, picked out a permanent capital and drafted the Bill of Rights.

In 1974, the House of Representatives consisted of considerably more than representatives. And although there were now 435 members, they made up only one part of the House, and sometimes not the most influential part. When you talk about the House today you must also talk about: committees, leaders, black members, female members, staffs, lobbyists, and more than 10,000 employees.

COMMITTEES

Committees as we know them today did not exist in 1789. A special or "select" committee was formed for every bill or legislative purpose. When it had completed its job it went out of business. By 1975 there were twenty-two permanent committees, a select committee on the aging, eight joint committees and a passel of nonsensical committees on everything from the parking garage to the House beauty parlor.

Which Committees Are Best for Members? On some, like Appropriations, Armed Services or Interior, a congressman will toil hard and long and be given an opportunity to assume some responsibility. Most of the work will be done on small subcommittees. On Ways and Means he'll be asked to attend many seemingly endless hearings before the full committee, sessions in which he'll be lucky to get five minutes of questioning of important witnesses. Ways and Means handles major legislation but until 1975 it had no subcommittees and was dominated by its chairman, Wilbur Mills. The opportunity for responsibility among the younger members, or for that matter, any individual was minimal. The only way to have fun on Ways and Means was to take on the establishment. For most of the other committees, like Commerce, Banking and Currency, or Education and Labor or Foreign Affairs, the degree of work depends on the willingness of the members to do it. Some actively participate in every set of hearings, others rarely attend anything but the key, publicized sessions.

Which Committees Are Best for Presidents of the United States? The Foreign Affairs Committee has always been popular with chief executives, Democratic or Republican. Until recently, the majority of the committee thought it impolite to interfere with a president's conduct of foreign policy. In 1972, former Secretary of State, Dean Rusk, testified before the committee. While waiting for the hearing to begin, he chatted with a few reporters at the press table. "You know," he said, "I've always liked this committee. They're good, responsible people." The committee was certainly good to the Johnson administration. How responsible it was is open to question. It wasn't until the summer of 1972, and then by the barest of margins, that the committee finally turned against the war in Vietnam.

Which Committees Are Best for Lobbyists? Ways and Means, with its tax and trade responsibilities, and Commerce with its jurisdiction over a wide range of business oriented legislation, offer promising possibilities for special interests. Under the chairmanship of Wilbur Mills at Ways and Means, and under Oren Harris and his successor, Harley Staggers, at Commerce, special interest lobbyists have usually batted better than .500. But for sheer, unmitigated take-overism, the championship has to go to the Merchant Marine Committee. For years, shipbuilders, operators and unions have plied the friendly waters of the committee, happily extracting hundreds of millions of dollars of government subsidies for the American merchant marine. There are arguments to be made in behalf of supporting the maritime industry. But there are also consumer and taxpayer arguments which hold that it doesn't have to be anywhere near the amount that has been forked over by Congress. You will rarely hear that point made in the Merchant and Fisheries Committee.

Which Committees Are Best for Newsmen? For getting information and stories, the wild and woolly committees, like Banking and Currency or Education and Labor, are hard to beat. In the past decade both have been marked by tumultuous and long-running brawls, usually between Democrats and Republicans but sometimes just among Democrats. A reporter covering Capitol Hill soon learns that his best chance for a story lies in such situations, where both sides want their version put before the public. Members are eager to fill in a newsman on a secret session, especially before an opponent gets to the reporter.

The Armed Services Committee is not nearly as contentious as these two but I found it more challenging. Although the committee has always been heavily weighted with promilitary people, there has always been a small but articulate minority publicizing the other side of the issue. And contrary to what you might expect, given its image and the national security claims it could hide behind, the committee is much less secretive about its business than most committees are. Its former chairman, the venerable Carl Vinson, established the open-door policy a long time ago, inviting newsmen to inspect the reports and correspondence the committee received from the Pentagon. Oneta Stockstill, who retired in 1974 as the panel's cheerful and competent executive secretary, kept the practice alive during the reigns of Vinson's successors.

There is something I call the "hard work syndrome" which afflicts individual members as well as committees. After legislators have spent months poring over reports, listening to witnesses and wrangling over the drafting of a bill, they don't take kindly to criticism of their accomplishments. They contend that the critics can't possibly know as much about the subject as they do, and if they did, and were intellectually honest, they would reach the same conclusions. What the committees do is equate hard work with good judgment. Almost everybody on Armed Services works hard. For weeks upon weeks every year, they meet morning and afternoon on the weapons procurement bill, listening to an endless stream of Pentagon officials explain why they need more of this new plane or more of that new missile. They ask questions and miss a lot of activities that would be a great deal more fun. But they frequently approach their task with a mind-set that blocks truly clear, objective thinking about the weapons system. The question shouldn't be how many missiles are needed but whether the missile itself is needed.

Besides legislating, committees are supposed to keep an eye on how government departments and agencies have been carrying out legislation already enacted. Most committees either are unable or unwilling to carry out their oversight responsibilities. The Federal Bureau of Investigation is a classic example. J. Edgar Hoover would not appear before any House committee except the appropriations subcommittee which handled his budget, and then only in closed session before a superfriendly chairman, John Rooney. Rooney wouldn't permit any tough questions to be asked of the director. After Hoover died, the country learned that the bureau was not as efficient and cohesive as he had led the Rooney subcommittee and the rest of the country to believe.

The Government Operations Committee is the principal investigative committee of the House. Its oversight record has been dismal. A few of its subcommittees have conducted decent investigations now and then but they were in spite of, rather than because of, the full committee chairmen, the late William Dawson and the recently retired Chet Holifield. Both men displayed an incredible reluctance to rock the boat—not necessarily because some special interest had gotten to them, but simply because they didn't want turmoil.

This lassitude of Democratic committees is especially ironic when you remember that since 1969 they have faced off against departments and agencies run by a Republican administration.

A longtime observer of the House explained the irony this way:

"For years the Democrats controlled committees and left the executive alone because a Democratic administration was in power. By the time Republicans took over, the Democrats had become so lethargic that they weren't able to summon up the killer instinct that Republicans have and which you need in order to conduct aggressive investigations."

This lethargy of Democratic committees is matched only by the lethargy of Democratic leaders. Together they produce Democratic ineptitude.

THE LEADERS

The Democrats have had a leadership problem ever since Sam Rayburn died in 1961. John McCormack took over in 1962 and enjoyed the leisure of Democratic administrations, which helped him get his troops in line for votes and precluded the need to launch an investigation of the bureaucracy. But McCormack still had his problems, not the least of which was his refusal to emerge from the New Deal, World War II and the postwar struggle against communism. When it came to domestic programs, he stood with the majority of his party in the House. But on the war in Vietnam, military spending, the flag, and dissent he sided with the conservative wing rather than with the northern liberals, the men and women who had become the mainstream of the Democratic party.

McCormack's heart was in the right place on social issues. Although those of us who were exposed to his speeches sometimes regarded them as the ramblings of an old man, he could be quite poignant when he would recall the poverty he saw as a boy and how it had left him with a concern for all poor and abused people. But by the time he became Speaker, he had already turned seventy, and whatever abilities he had did not add up to forceful and innovative leadership.

McCormack's successor, Carl Albert, was a man of exceptional ability—before he became Speaker. The predictions of greatness that accompanied his ascension to power in 1971 never materialized. Carl Albert had no stomach for the job after he landed it. Though more intelligent and sophisticated than McCormack, Albert also maintained a cold war mentality about Vietnam that alienated many of the liberals. On the other hand, his accommodations to the left—such as his concessions to the black caucus—irritated the conservatives. His job certainly has not been easy, but he did little to gain sympathy. Personally he has not been close to many members and he has shunned the press, through which he might have been able, for example, to explain the quandary he faced on Vietnam, torn as he was between his own convictions and his party leadership responsibilities.

It might be said that Republicans have been lucky with their leaders. Yet it's not luck. Instead of relying on the orderly leadership ladder of succession—and luck—as the Democrats had, the GOP decided in 1965 that its leadership wasn't doing the job. So a band of middle-aged turks threw out Charlie Halleck and moved Gerald Ford into the top leadership spot, backing him up with Melvin Laird and John Rhodes. When Laird left for the Defense Department secretaryship in 1969, he was replaced by John Anderson. All are men of high political competence and some possess even greater attributes. Interestingly, they also have played key roles in national Republican politics, something their counterparts have never done in the Democratic party.

Considering that they were usually woefully outnumbered, Ford and his team won more than their share of battles. Of course, it's easier to oppose than to propose, but the fact remains that they handled their tasks with competence. The same could not be said of the Democratic leaders.

BLACK MEMBERS, WOMEN MEMBERS

Nineteen seventy-three in the House might well have been called the Year of Blacks and Women. The Ninety-third Congress contained a record number of Negro representatives—fifteen. And if the sixteen female lawmakers did not set a record,* they topped anything racked up by their predecessors in terms of the splash they made in the media and the attention they drew from the public.

But numbers and notoriety are not the best ways to measure the impact of either group. Where those individuals were positioned and what they were doing with the power at their disposal were the telling points. In some instances their performances were disappointing, the publicity and

* The old record, set in 1962, was seventeen. It was topped by the 1974 elections, which sent eighteen women to the House. The same elections established a new record for the number of black representatives in the House—sixteen. The figures for blacks do not include Walter Fauntroy, the Negro nonvoting delegate from the District of Columbia.

statistics notwithstanding. In other cases, the surface evidence did not give full credit to their accomplishments.

Rep. Charles Diggs of Detroit took over chairmanship of the District of Columbia Committee in 1973, and before the year ended he had steered through the House a bill granting the (mostly black) citizens of Washington a substantial degree of home rule, something blacks and liberals had been trying unsuccessfully to do for one hundred years. Diggs also retained his chairmanship of the African subcommittee on the Foreign Affairs Committee, a post from which he skillfully began to build an African lobby, as it were, the one place in the U.S. government where black Africa felt sure someone would go to bat for its interests.

In 1969, black House members decided that individual achievement and acquisition of power were not enough. Collective action was also necessary. That year they formed the Congressional Black Caucus, an organization open to all Negro representatives and dedicated to focusing congressional and national attention on issues of importance to black America as well as advancing legislative remedies to problems stemming from those issues.

Soon the caucus was churning out press releases and position papers, staging an annual fund-raising dinner and generally catching the notice of the media and black political and intellectual circles around the country. But it wasn't bringing about much change in the House or in the Nixon administration. The caucus discovered that no matter how stinging its indictments, how eloquent its pronouncements, it couldn't hope to shame what it regarded as an unsympathetic administration into seriously and compassionately addressing itself to the needs of black and poor people. It also learned that 15 votes out of 435 didn't provide a hell of a lot of leverage and that fewer bills than imagined lent themselves to the kind of vote swapping that generates political clout.

Shortly before the Ninety-third Congress convened in January, 1973, members of the caucus met and took stock of their institution. "They realized they couldn't be all things to all people," recalled former Executive Director Gus Adair. They decided to leave noncongressional causes to other groups and to work their own territory, trying harder to influence legislation and to inject a black concern into those congressional activities that, while not necessarily leading to a legislative outcome, do leave an imprint on government policy.

Thus, even before the House organized itself for the Ninety-third Congress, a caucus delegation marched over to the Capitol to see Speaker Albert to insist that Ronald Dellums be appointed to one of the vacancies on the Armed Services Committee. Despite the protestations of Committee Chairman F. Edward Hébert, Albert complied. The caucus had succeeded in planting the first black ever on the Armed Services Committee. And not only had it put a black there, but it had placed the black of its choice, the black member with the most militant, radical and activist image, the black from Berkeley, California. The Pentagon added the name of Dellums to its list of congressmen slated for special care, the lawmakers who rate the high level intelligence briefings, the ingratiating attentions of admirals and generals.

In the ensuing months the caucus squeezed its voting power to the last drop, keeping a watchful eye out for any closely fought legislative battles where its members' support would be appreciated and repaid. Leading the group now was Louis Stokes, who with his brother Carl earned his political stripes fighting in the trenches of Cleveland's

Democratic organization. When the farm bloc was resisting an effort to impose a $20,000 ceiling on subsidies, several black congressmen from urban districts came through with votes for the agriculture interests. They found themselves siding with conservatives and opposing liberals.

"My people couldn't care less about farm issues," Stokes later told a visitor. "And if they do I explain that we're now playing the same game they (white politicians) have always played. That's how you get things done. In this case, we got paid back on the minimum wage bill, which does mean a lot to my constituents." When Albert put his personal prestige on the line and appealed for votes in behalf of his cherished extension of the Capitol's west front, black congressmen remembered the Dellums episode and many voted with him. "The Speaker had been good to us," Stokes observed.

In 1973 an experienced lobbyist for liberal causes gave the black caucus a mixed review.

"They've not been terribly effective. But there haven't been that many opportunities. They just don't have that much voting power. Where they have been effective is within their own party. They've managed to spread the black members around on committees instead of bunching them up on a few. I think you'll see them becoming increasingly influential within the Democratic caucus. With sixteen blacks and a lot of white Democratic liberals who march to the black tune on black issues, they can be powerful. Along the same line, watch them after a Democrat gets back in the White House."

The same lobbyist gave high marks to Stokes and St. Louis's William Clay for political savvy. He faulted the black caucus for not taking a more active interest in 1973's reshaping of the congressional budget decision process and for doing next to nothing about the woeful lack of blacks on committee staffs. Charles Rangel, Adam Clayton Powell's successor from Harlem, took over the caucus chairmanship in 1974 and demonstrated that he too rated political skill over rhetoric.

Probably the greatest tribute to the caucus' record of accomplishment came from Armed Services Committee Chairman Hébert. Still smarting over the Dellums appointment months after it had been made, Hébert was asked how he thought the House's Democratic leadership was doing.

"Leadership! Ha! The black caucus is running the leadership."

ぱ

Women members have rarely acted collectively and have eschewed formation of a permanent group made up of all the women in the House or even all the women of one party. Individually they've been moving up the seniority ladder into positions of influence, and occasionally they have employed that power to further the goals of a women's issue. The Equal Rights Amendment would have received a favorable vote on the floor even if there had been no female members in the House, but getting the measure to the floor was largely due to the dogged determination and legislative skill of Martha Griffiths. And it was Mrs. Griffiths who virtually browbeat her male colleagues in 1964 into accepting a floor amendment that added sex as one of the conditions of employment prohibited by the Civil Rights Act. (Or, as she likes to phrase it, "I put sex in the Civil Rights Act.")

Yet sadly, the overall performance of women members has not matched the headlines captured by such colorful personalities as fiery Bella Abzug and pretty Patricia

Schroeder. Their ranks have included a few exceptional legislators, a few who were dismal and too many who ranged from acceptable to mediocre. In short, they did about as well as their male colleagues. The only difference was that the public viewed male members with a healthy ration of cynicism; they expected more from women members, assuming that the women must have been extra special to have broken barriers and entered into the predominantly male club.

Republican female members have generally acted as if they belonged to their party's women's auxiliary, not entitled to speak or participate as fully as their male colleagues. Most seemed satisfied to play the role of smiling clubwomen, cheerfully following directions and going along with the team. Since 1963 the only assertive Republican women I can recall are ex-Reps. Frances Bolton of Ohio and Katherine St. George of New York, both of them rich and confident dowagers, and Margaret Heckler, a feisty GOP moderate from Massachusetts. Most of the others behaved as though plunging into debate or tangling with an opponent would be unladylike.

Occasionally a female member, just as a male lawmaker might do, will use the House to achieve a goal outside of the House. Bella Abzug needed a nationally spotlighted pulpit from which to rally support for the antiwar movement, feminism and the other social issues she espoused. Although her personality and style alienated many members and diminished her effectiveness during her first two years, she began to win grudging admiration for her willingness to master the rules of the House, learn the tricks of legislation and, in the parlance of Washington, to do her homework before she took the floor.

On the other hand, Ella Grasso, wearing an old sweater, glasses perched on her forehead, seemed to do little more than sit in the House chamber, looking like a tired, aging housewife. She cared little about advancing in the House or achieving national notoriety. But from the time she arrived in 1971 she regularly sent press releases back to Connecticut, went home often, saw a lot of voters and when 1974 rolled around she was the frontrunner and eventual winner in her state's governorship race.

Shirley Chisholm was another woman who decided that the House was more useful for what could be done outside the institution than inside. Capitalizing on her publicized status as the first black woman member of Congress, she made her run for the Democratic presidential nomination. She toured the lecture circuit. She became a heroine and model for women, black as well as white, encouraging un-known numbers to enter politics. Yet the country's gain was the House's loss. For Shirley Chisholm could have made one hell of a legislator.

She had the gift of dramatic presence, which in itself was remarkable. No doubt, she looked like she could keep a classroom of children in their place—straightbacked and bony, offering a smile, ready with a frown—but intimidat-ing a legislature full of seasoned male politicians? Not this middle-aged woman with the high-pitched voice, the slight speech defect, the neatly curled hair, the sparkling bright blouses. This old-fashioned Negro churchlady a fiery spokesman of the radical left? Never. And yet it was this unique combination of middle-class propriety and count-er-culture rhetoric that threw her colleagues off balance. Underneath the primness they sensed the hissing of a volcano.

On the night of November 4, 1971, the volcano erupted. Emotions had been boiling all evening. Members were de-bating an antibusing amendment, a subject which in 1971 guaranteed acrimony under ideal conditions. On this night, conditions were anything but ideal. Turning the debate especially bitter was the performance of Michigan members. Reeling under the impact of a massive court-ordered busing plan handed down by a federal judge in Detroit, the former battlers for civil rights were now supporting curbs on busing. One of them even put forth an amendment to prohibit the kind of integration plan that had been ordered for Detroit and its suburbs.

Into this cauldron stepped Mrs. Chisholm. She had been sitting quietly and listening—and burning. Finally she stood, was recognized and walked to the rostrum. A hush came over the House. Even the noisy backbenchers seemed to sense this was no time for skylarking.

And she let them have it. Looking directly at them, she called her fellow lawmakers—southerners and northerners —hypocrites. The sentences burst upon them in salvos of staccato fury.

"Racism is so inherent in the bloodstream of this country that you cannot see beyond a particular limit.

"You are only concerned when whites are affected.

"I say to the members: where were you when the black children were being bused right past the white schools in the community?

"Come out from behind your mask."

Suddenly, she had stopped attacking and was pleading.

"Forget they are white children.

"Forget they are black children.

"Just remember one thing.

"They are America's children."

Her allies stood and applauded. The targets of her words sat as they had sat during her speech—silently, uncomfortably, like schoolboys enduring a teacher's tonguelashing. Mrs. Chisholm did not win that night. History's greatest orator could not have won. But this second-term lady lawmaker had demonstrated to establishment members that they were dealing with a unique property, a radical who brought with her the sense of timing that southern Democrats learned early in the game. No typical liberal overkill here. She spoke only when the moment was right. Otherwise she sat upright and listened, letting her reputation do the rest.

The potential for greatness in the House was there, but Mrs. Chisholm chose to ignore the opportunity. Instead she worked the larger arena, crusading throughout the country in behalf of blacks, women, the poor and, in the opinion of some critics, to feed the growing ego of Shirley Chisholm. It culminated in her run for the 1972 Democratic presidential nomination, an adventure which inscribed her in history as the first black woman presidential candidate and which undoubtedly did much for the psyches of black and white women. But it also collided with, and pretty well shattered, visions of black politicians for a unified black political strategy that election year.

Mrs. Chisholm's rejection of the House as a career followed what she perceived as the House's rejection of her—both as Shirley Chisholm and as any new member anxious to get moving. Soon after arriving she drew her committee assignment: Agriculture. She blew up, interpreting the move as a slap at her and her constituents. What kind of sadistic practical jokers would name the representative of Bedford Stuyvesant, one of America's most overwhelming city slums, to the Agriculture Committee?

Her anger was understandable. On the surface, the action by the leadership and the Democratic Committee on Committees seemed ludicrous. But she wasn't the first New York liberal to suffer such a fate in her freshman year.

Others put in two years on the committee and then moved on to a more desirable assignment. They also discovered that the Agriculture Committee extended marvelous opportunities for the activist congressman interested in welfare and consumer issues. At one time or another, the committee held jurisdiction over the food stamp, school milk, school lunch, surplus food, meat inspection and pesticide programs, all of which were activities that affected far more city dwellers—like those living in Bedford Stuyvesant—than farmers.

But Mrs. Chisholm brushed aside the counsel of those who urged her to stay on Agriculture and refused to accept the assignment. The leadership yielded, at least for face-saving purposes, and named her to the Veterans Committee. At first glance the concerns of that panel, what with its American Legion aura, would appear to be as irrelevant to Mrs. Chisholm and her constituents as those of the Agriculture Committee. In fact, the Veterans Committee offered a sufficiently aroused legislator a chance to raise hell about the miserly GI bill and other inadequate government programs that greeted the hundreds of thousands of black and other Vietnam veterans. Unfortunately, Mrs. Chisholm passed up the chance, taking little interest in the committee or its work.

In 1971, at the start of her second term, she snared a seat on the Education and Labor Committee, reportedly in exchange for her support of the late Hale Boggs in his successful race for majority leader. The jurisdiction of the committee—day care and other antipoverty programs, education, equal opportunity laws—fit her longtime interests and the needs of her district. Yet Mrs. Chisholm was soon to discover that she was just another liberal on a committee overloaded with liberals. Few issues arose before the committee in which her vote or actions would make much difference in the outcome of any battle. By 1974, she indicated she was losing interest in the House.

Two new women members with enormous potential caught the nation's attention through the televising of the Judiciary Committee's impeachment inquiry and its hearing on President Ford's pardon of Richard Nixon. But even before the panel went on television, perceptive observers had pegged as comers Elizabeth Holtzman of Brooklyn and Barbara Jordan, the black congresswoman from Houston. Rep. Holtzman, the audacious and humorless interrogator of President Ford, had arrived in the House in 1973 after ousting longtime Judiciary Committee Chairman Emanuel Celler in the Democratic primary. Caring little about image or media notice, she kept her eyes open, her mind operating overtime, worked prodigiously and pushed more legislation through the House than any freshman in recent memory. Meanwhile, Rep. Jordan, whose eloquence fixed her as one of the stars of the impeachment debate, had already impressed her colleagues by tempering her doctrinaire liberalism with a keenly developed intelligence and an abundance of political know-how, much of it gained from her experience in the Texas State Senate.

THE STAFF

Several thousand people fall into this category in the House. It includes administrative assistants to congressmen as well as their legislative assistants, press aides and secretaries. It includes the lawyers and other experts on committee staffs, the accountants and administrators who work for the clerk and sergeant at arms, the engineers and architects who are assigned to the Capitol architect. As you might expect, they come in different political hues and they present a rich variety in style of operation.

Edie Johnson works the front desk at the reception room of the House Armed Services Committee. Trim, attractive, seasoned, she was divorced a number of years ago from an air force officer. She spends a nonstop day shuffling Pentagon officials, defense industry lobbyists, reporters and congressmen in and out of the complex of offices and hearing rooms that the committee has scattered throughout the Rayburn Building. In between, she and one or two other staffers working with her may field up to fifty calls an hour. The calls come from congressional offices, the Pentagon, lobbyists, newsmen and the public. Almost all of them want information—what's happening to a particular investigation, what's in a bill, where the legislation stands right now. Edie Johnson comes through for all but the most cantankerous of her callers. Sometimes during the day she must amass reports on what the chairman, the subcommittees and the staff have been doing so that she can fill in not only the telephone callers but also the *Congressional Record*, the *Daily Legislative Calendar* and the computerized bill status system. It leaves her ragged by midafternoon. Call her and find out.

"It's ruined my personality, made me mean as hell. By 4:30 I'm crotchety. I guess I've been at it too long. Hold on. (Click. You're on hold. Minutes tick by. Click. We're back again.) Oh Christ. All four lines are going now. Can you call me later?"

That's the front office of the Armed Services Committee. Hidden from public view, alongside the committee's hearing room is a wing of comfortable, well-appointed and spacious offices—extremely spacious by House standards, run-of-the-mill for a government agency—that house the staff professionals. The atmosphere here is busy but not frantic.

Other than staff people from other offices in the Rayburn Building, few people enter here without an appointment or first checking in at the front office.

Occupying the first office in the line is Bernice Kalinowski, a secretary. Next to her is her boss and the boss of everybody else on the committee, Frank Slatinshek, chief counsel.

He is neat, well-organized, hardworking, and has developed the skill most important to a staff director: he is amiable and agreeable to all of the forty-one committee members but dutiful to the chairman. The current chairman, F. Edward Hébert, considers Slatinshek "a genius." Slatinshek has been able to translate Hébert's sometimes flamboyant policy decisions into well-focused, thorough hearings and investigations. Over the years the professional relationship has evolved into a social one as well, and now Slatinshek is one of the few Hill people that Hébert says he sees after working hours.

John Ford is another aide that Hébert leans on. A former reporter, Ford currently holds the staff's unofficial chair as resident intellectual, a post he inherited from an ex-staffer who also read extensively, could recite poetry and was able to conduct entertaining conversations with reporters and others who might not be as taken with the military as the committee was. He erases a stereotype, contradicting the notion that by definition a staff member of the Armed Services Committee is a raving militarist.

Because Ford's political and public relation instincts are sharp, Hébert relies on him for a variety of services, from helping to develop strategy for fights on the House floor or in conferences with the Senate to writing speeches. He's also become an expert on NATO defenses and recomputation of retired military pay, a goal which the committee has steadfastly resisted (and for which it has not received the credit due it from liberals and all taxpayers, considering the billions that recomputation would add to the Pentagon budget).

Bill Broydrick is also into the military. But he works for Democratic Rep. Les Aspin of Wisconsin. Because Aspin has built a career out of catching the military on goofs, Broydrick spends most of his time trying to nail or embarrass the Pentagon. The rest of his time he spends trying to nail other government departments or corporations he and Aspin suspect of taking the citizenry. Broydrick has been doing this since late 1971 and he's become very good at it. What's remarkable is that in 1974 he was only twenty-five. Six months after signing on with Aspin he learned more about getting his boss's name in the paper and uncorking bottled-up information than most congressional assistants will ever know.

Broydrick is not cool. Nor neat. He is a disheveled, black-haired kid with a grinning Irish face, glasses and a tie that is always awry. He operates out of an office that was made to order for him. It's on the fifth floor of the old Cannon Building, about as far away as you can get from the seats of power in the House and still claim membership. Half the fifth floor is an attic. One side of the corridors is lined with caged storage bins. The other side is lined with offices, the offices of junior members, like Aspin, who aren't hung up on a status location, who are willing to trade prestige for a bit of extra space.

For some reason Aspin's office doesn't look like it got the space bonus. Rooms and half rooms are crammed with desks, files, boxes and piles of paper on the floor. People seem physically trapped at their desks. The girls are wearing jeans. Everybody smiles. The place has a madcap quality about it.

I ask Broydrick a question. He picks up a telephone. He asks my question.

We hear a female voice on the other side of the three-quarter-length partition: "Tim, Bill wants to know what day flight pay was on the floor. Do you remember?"

A short pause. We hear a male voice on the other side of the partition. "It was February twenty-first."

"February twenty-first," says a female voice from the other side of the partition.

"Right, thanks," says Broydrick to the phone. He turns to me. "February twenty-first."

From a newsman's point of view, a congressman's aide is valuable if he can speak for his boss, if, as someone once said, he holds his man's proxy. Without having to check with his boss can he tell a reporter—either on or off the record—how his congressman is reacting to trouble in the committee, a political battle back home? A lot of administrative assistants—AA's, they're called on the Hill—hold the proxy. When they do they're valuable. They're loaded with information and fun to talk to.

There's nothing quite comparable to them in the executive branch, where most officials close to the top are either inaccessible, scared to death that they're exceeding their authority or simply aren't privy to everything their boss is up to. That's not true in the House where a good AA or press aide deals at length with the congressman every day, has coffee with him in the morning and a drink with him in the evening.

In between chats with the member and chats with the newsmen, AA's plow through the nitty gritty of congressional work. It's a profession that demands a generalist with a host of specialties. They've got to know how to put together and stick to a budget, manage an office, develop legislation, attend to casework and solve political problems. In a vague sort of way I sensed what an AA did for a living but I didn't get a true feel for the job until I asked an AA I know to keep a log of what he did on a particular day. Following is the log of Marshall Lynam, an ex-newspaperman who has been with Rep. Jim Wright, a Democrat from Ft. Worth, Texas, since 1961.

Day's Log

7:35 A.M.—Arrive at office, scan first of five deliveries of mail.

8:10—Go to breakfast in Rayburn cafeteria, read *Washington Post*.

8:46—Call staff member who is ill at home; read mail.

9:20—Answer call from spokesman for contractors' association about fuel requirements in energy legislation.

9:30—Answer call from congressman on Armed Services Committee who is anxious to talk to Jim Wright when he gets out of meeting.

9:34—Talk in office with committee staff man about bridge investigation requested by Jim Wright.

9:40—Answer call from constituent about requirements of Capitol page school.

9:50—Answer call from fraternal organization who wants help in locating Texas expert on the elderly.

10:22—Answer call from truckers' association about 55 MPH speed limit.

10:50—Answer call from Jim Wright about scheduled radio appearance.

1 P.M.—Lunch in Rayburn cafeteria with committee staff man on bridge investigation.

1:15—Talk in office with another committee staff man about photo equipment.

2:30—Talk in office with job applicant.

2:45—Call third committee staff man about upcoming hearings on water pollution.

3:10—Answer call inquiring about proper name of railroad in Fort Worth.

3:31—Answer call from newsman about Jim Wright's thinking on public financing of elections.

3:37—Talk in office with secretary about air reservations on trip to Texas.

3:40—Talk again with staff man on bridge investigation.

4:10—Call VA to try to assist a veteran who needs medical treatment.

4:11—Call another VA office on same case.

4:20—Talk in office with secretary about handling of report on nursing home.

4:30—Assist Congressman Wright in taping of weekly radio report.

5:25—Answer call from friend about invitation to reception.

5:30—Answer call from businessman about forthcoming Jim Wright speech.

5:40—Answer call from congressman and work out time for him to talk with Jim Wright.

5:45—Answer call from religious broadcast organization about radio speech by Jim Wright.

6:30—Call Jim Wright in cloakroom about scheduled reception.

In between time, worked on mail and reports.

What keeps congressional offices busiest is what is known on the Hill as casework—the constituent who is trying to get a relative into a veterans' hospital, the retiree who is not getting his full Social Security benefits, the mother who's worried about her son in the army. The congressman, or those acting in his name, takes on the role of ombudsman, serving as agent for citizens who would otherwise be stymied or intimidated by a mammoth and awesome bureaucracy. Ironically, the more programs Congress enacts the more it brings upon itself. There was no Medicare correspondence file in 1964. In 1974 there was one and it contained several bulging folders.

Bill Steponkus is a burly, good-natured former reporter (journalists, with their generalized backgrounds and their interest in politics seem to slide easily into congressional staff jobs) who serves as AA for Charles Whalen, a liberal Republican from Dayton, Ohio. Whalen used to be an economics professor and tends to be more issue oriented than most members. That produces more mail than there would be if Whalen was a casework congressman, one whose office was dedicated primarily to serving the constituents.

"The work just keeps piling on," says Steponkus. "Call it empire building if you want to but it's there. We now have staff authorization for sixteen people. In five years it will be up to twenty. We hope mechanization will keep pace. If we do get four more people, we'll probably put two of them back in the district. We just won't have the room here. We're already farming out some work to the district.

"Why is the load increasing? Because we're getting more mail. We're getting more casework correspondence as well as more issue mail. The boost in the casework is pretty understandable. I'm not as sure of the reason for the other. I suspect it has something to do with the grass root movements that have developed. You know, 'Write Your Congressman' ads, Common Cause, well-orchestrated campaigns on all sorts of subjects. I'm not sure we're getting that much more individually inspired mail. But whatever it is, I think they deserve a thoughtful and complete answer. Hell, the guy is a constituent.

"If the issue is one on which we've gotten a great deal of mail, we'll have to send back a form letter. But it will be a form letter that represents the thinking of the boss and it will have a lot in it.

"Some of these other offices are able to appear so quiet and orderly because they don't go in for our kind of approach. They'll get mail and send a generalized reply. You know, 'Dear So and So. I appreciate your views on the subject of abortion. It has been a concern of mine for some time. I am happy to have your input for my consideration. I appreciate the time you have taken. Please continue to keep me advised. Sincerely yours, etc.' "

LOBBYISTS

He was a Washington lobbyist for a large corporation. He had been in the business for a few years, was good at his job and still young enough so that a future with his company looked bright. We sat in a restaurant and I asked him to tell me about lobbying.

"I enjoy the competition. I like it when I can go out and whip a guy's ass. I mean a guy from competing industry. And occasionally a committee staff man who has been giving me a hard time. By whipping, I mean getting the committee or the House or Senate going our way. I think my track record is about 50 percent, which for around here is pretty good. My company knows I can't produce miracles."

He acknowledged that sometimes he has to reach far to accomplish an important objective. It happened once in 1973 over a bill which was of crucial interest to his corporation. The committee handling the legislation was evenly split on the measure but he found a member who personally and politically didn't care which way it went. And he was for rent.

"We struck a bargain. I said I'd raise some campaign money for him. On April 6, the day before the new campaign reporting law went into effect, I turned over to him a cashier's check for well over $10,000, made out to the treasurer of his D.C. committee.* Hell, he didn't even know who his treasurer was. Well, we got his vote in committee and on the floor but when the bill got to conference he said he wanted something else. He said he wanted us to use our influence with the administration and get this guy on his staff a job with the————Department. He wanted the guy out so he could use part of his salary to increase the pay of a secretary on his staff whom he had been shacking up with. With the extra money she could get them an apartment. We couldn't do it and he gave us trouble. He had said if we didn't come through he'd take the Senate position in conference, which would be a disaster for us. It turned out that we dug up a guy on the Senate side who owed us a favor so we came out of it all right.

"I felt sorry about one thing. The guy I was up against, another lobbyist, was a good man. But I beat him and it set back his career. He's still got his job but he's not going any higher. I'm sorry about that because he's a nice guy and he was good at his job."

He said he had never been asked to get women for a congressman. "But I know a lobbyist who specializes in it and word gets around. This guy does a lot with one House committee chairman. He travels a lot with him and a couple of broads. Me, I confine my socializing to drinking with staff guys. And though I enjoy it, I still consider it business.

* At the time, District of Columbia election law did not require that the identity of campaign contributors be disclosed.

"No, I don't do anything I'm particularly ashamed of. When my company benefits, the communities in which we're located benefit too. Jobs are at stake. I have to be nice to people I sometimes don't think much of but that doesn't bother me. If it's a shit I'm dealing with, I simply regard him as a business object. Besides, I figure for another five years I can eat crow. Then I can move into big money with my company."

That's one kind of lobbyist. Relatively rough. Unusually honest with himself. There are others with different techniques. And there are others who operate on a different plane altogether. Some observations about lobbyists:

■ Not all of them are cynical or mercenary. Many believe in what they're doing and are convinced that if they are successful the country will be better off. This includes those representing special business interests as well as those representing citizens' groups, like Common Cause, The NAACP, groups for abortion and groups against abortion.

■ Although the point is a bit over-emphasized by congressmen, lobbyists do provide useful information about an issue, at least one side of an issue. If the member listens to lobbyists from both camps, he has been exposed to the best spokesmen and is in a relatively good position to reach a judgment based on the merits.

■ Lobbyists perform services for congressmen—like doing their work for them. Toward the last two years of the Vietnam war debate, Common Cause lobbyists David Cohen and Fred Wertheimer not only directed their organization's program of corralling House votes but literally wrote antiwar amendments and devised parliamentary strategy. Similarly, General Dynamics officials wrote some of the speeches delivered by House members when critics of the F-111 tried unsuccessfully to legislate a cutback in production of the controversial fighter-bomber.

■ The most effective lobbies are those which represent a great many people or a fair number of people strategically scattered about the country. Like schoolchildren and federal workers.

Not long ago the Appropriations Committee got a jolt when the House ignored the recommendations of the august committee and topped by a few hundred million dollars the amount of money the panel had recommended for aid to education that year. Behind the upset was a newly formed lobby of public and private educators—teachers, principals, curriculum specialists, administrators, superintendents, state education department officials. They combined their considerable resources, set up an office in a Capitol Hill hotel, hired a crackerjack ex-Senate staffer who had specialized in education to run it and then went about buttonholing their local congressmen. Since every congressional district is a recipient of some school aid from Washington, the results were predictable. The alternative to more federal money would have been a cutback in school services or a hike in local taxes.

Federal workers are not permitted to strike; that doesn't particularly bother them. They've got something better going for them. Over the past decade, employee unions have built a pipeline to the House and Senate Civil Service committees, through which they've been sending a message understood by every politician: you take care of us and we'll take care of you. There were approximately 2.8 million civilians working for the federal government in 1974. More importantly they were located in every congressional district, and many of them had spouses and voting age children who had a vital stake in their economic welfare. All were acutely aware of how their congressmen voted on civil service pay-raise bills. Unions have also managed to raise campaign money for friendly congressmen. The upshot has been that the federal employee, once a stepchild of our economy, has not only achieved long desired "comparability" with his private sector counterpart but now frequently surpasses him in salary and benefits.

A small but well-organized special interest can bowl over a disorganized, flabby majority, no matter how popular its cause. Public opinion surveys are constantly telling us that a decisive majority of the American people would accept tightened controls on gun ownership. But the gun lobby, led by the National Rifle Association, has effectively managed to limit firearms legislation to the minimum.

Camp safety is a goal that it seems would please everyone. Yet in 1971 the House rejected a worthwhile camp safety bill sent to it by the House Education and Labor Committee and substituted a meaningless measure pushed by camp operators including, of all people, the Boy Scouts of America. The camps didn't want to bear the expense of buying life jackets and other safety measures the bill would have required. Rep. Bob Eckhardt of Texas, a sensitive and decent congressman, wrote a letter of commiseration to Mitch Kurman, the father of a boy lost in a camping accident and the driving force behind the legislation. It was letter tinged with despair. "I sometimes fear . . . that the power of the special interest lobby groups to defeat propeople programs is limitless."

In 1789 the House was an assembly of individuals. By 1974 it had become an institution, one to which thousands of people including members, had dedicated their careers.

It is no longer the vibrant, dynamic reflection of the national will that its creators intended it to be. It has become an establishment unto itself, possessed of its own attitudes, approaches and responses to the changes and problems that arise in the United States. It has developed a working relationship with the bureaucracy, with corporate interest and with nonprofit interests. Simultaneously its members have developed to a fine art the technique of winning reelection without necessarily serving their constituents' interests.

5

The City within a City

THERE IS ONE policeman for every sixteen inhabitants of Congress. That makes the representatives, senators and staff members the most closely protected group of people in the United States, maybe anywhere in the world, outside of national leaders and the Pope. The protectors are congressional employees too. They constitute the U.S. Capitol police, a force of more than officers, assigned the single mission of safeguarding people and property found on the 155 acres of Capitol grounds. This seeming bit of trivia is offered for two reasons: (1) to illustrate how a city within a city has evolved on Capitol Hill and (2) to point up what Congress can really do when it sets its mind to the task, to wit: grow. Grow massively. Both points can also be made with the aid of a fantasy.

A military junta stages a successful *coup* in the United States. Congress is dissolved. The tradition of representative government is dealt a near mortal blow.

The event also plunges the Washington metropolitan area into a disastrous economic depression. A conservative

estimate is that upwards of 25,000 people are thrown out
of work. Besides the 535 members of the House and Senate,
the ranks of the jobless would include the 17,000 or so men
and women who work at the Capitol; the approximately
5,200 accountants; analysts and others toiling at Congress's
principal supporting agency, the General Accounting
Office (GAO); scores of newsmen who would be hard
pressed to justify their continued employment in Washington; hundreds of lobbyists representing special interests, public interests and foreign interests; more than
a thousand congressional liaison officials and legislative
draftsmen scattered throughout government; and an un-
told number of workers in the private sector who provide
Congress with services, deliver goods and build things for
it.

Some would cheer at the development. They include
Capitol Hill residents, who would be able to park on the
cleared streets, and cab drivers. Under a congressionally
drawn zone system, taxis in 1974 could charge only eighty-
five cents to transport a fare from the Hill to downtown, a
ride which during the day can tie them up for twenty minutes or more.

House members enjoy knocking the bureaucracy, but by
bureaucracy they mean the people and agencies operating
out of the *executive* branch of the federal government. Im-
plicit in their disparaging attitude is the contention that
the House fields a lean and hard work force, one that cuts
through red tape, gets things done and knows the value of
a taxpayer's dollar.

In truth, the House and Senate have spawned a bureaucracy of their own, one which proportionately rivals the
executive branch in overstaffing, money spent on itself
and generating inertia. Furthermore, the congressional
bureaucracy is unfettered by the kind of fiscal restraints
which the president, his budget managers and Congress im-

pose on the spending proposals of the departments and agencies. The Office of Management and Budget wouldn't dare look at, much less tamper with, the annual legislative appropriation. Congress reciprocates by pretty much giving the president carte blanche in drafting his budget for the White House. One result of this cozy arrangement has been a staggering growth explosion over the past ten years which has wiped out any quaint history-book images of elected representatives gathering together in a chamber to vote their constituents' wishes, applying *their* wisdom to solving the nation's problems and then packing up and going back home.

Figures tell the story better than any words:

■ Approximately 10,500 people, from a masseur to cabinet makers, work for the House of Representatives. Another 6,500 work at the Senate. The Government Printing Office employs some 8,500 persons and the Library of Congress another 4,000. Both agencies however, while part of the legislative branch, perform many government-wide and national functions (and thus would probably survive our fantasized coup).

■ The annual House payroll for the fiscal year starting July 1, 1974, totaled approximately $135 million.

■ The total bill for running the legislative branch the previous year, fiscal 1974, totaled $605 million. In fiscal 1964 the figure was only $214 million. It's a minor part of the federal budget but the ten-year jump amounted to more than 180 percent. In the same period, appropriations for strictly congressional operations—the House, Senate and Capitol—soared from $120 million (which included a sizable payment for the Rayburn Building) in 1964 to $297 million in 1974, an increase of 147 percent.

Looking at growth from another perspective, the size of the congressional budget climbed an average of less than 5 percent annually during the Korean War while during ten years of U.S. military involvement in Indochina it went up an average of 18.2 percent a year.

It has become a virtual shibboleth among reformers that Congress desperately needs more people and resources to help it compete with and keep a check on the executive branch. More staff. More computers. More information. How, they ask, can an Armed Services Committee staff of twelve professionals hope to effectively dissect a massive Pentagon budget prepared by hundreds of Defense Department employees, appraise weapons systems and investigate ongoing military activities? The answer is: fairly well—if the committee members want it to. And a second answer: if there aren't enough staff people, there's nothing to stop the House from hiring a lot more.

Indeed, Congress has amply demonstrated that money is no object when it decides that a Capitol Hill activity requires beefing up. Overkill is the usual outcome and the 1971 bombing of a Capitol washroom is a classic case in point. The response to that act of terrorism (which by 1974 was still unsolved) was immediate and overpowering. When the dust (of the reaction, not the explosion) settled two years later, Congress had fashioned itself a police force that, on a per capita basis, may be the largest and one of the best equipped in the world.

In a crash recruiting program, its numbers were bolstered by 377, enabling it to reach a 1974 level of more than a thousand officers. The additional personnel cost $4 million a year, boosting annual police expenses to $12.3 million. Three million dollars was provided for a sophisticated security system. It includes X-ray equipment for inspecting the parcels and briefcases of persons entering congressional facilities and a detection system which incorporates night fighting measures developed in Vietnam and the latest in sports telecasting techniques. As explained by Capitol Architect George White to the legislative appropriations subcommittee, an intruder in an unpatrolled corridor would set off the motion detection system. A policeman at a monitoring station could trail the suspicious entrant until he came within range of a closed circuit TV camera, whereupon he could be taped for "instant replay." And this, White proudly pointed out, could be used as evidence in court.

Through no fault of their own, the Capitol police were expanded, streamlined, modernized and militarized. The process stands as a classic congressional example of "hang the cost, full speed ahead." The results are both visual and statistical:

Visually—Any weekday morning while Congress is in session glance over the plaza below the east front of the Capitol and count the number of cops wedged in between the employees' parked cars. On the way to work one morning I did and found fourteen officers and one police car on duty there. The kindest thing that could be said about their usefulness was that they were serving as watchful parking lot attendants, seeing to it that tourists and others didn't grab an employee's or a newsman's parking space. A good deal of their time was spent in group bull sessions.

Drop into almost any committee or subcommittee hearing and the odds are you'll find one or two cops outside. It used to be that a cop was necessary to make sure reporters and/or spies didn't listen in at the door of closed sessions dealing with national security material. Then police were posted at other, nonclassified hearings to see to it that demonstrators didn't disrupt proceedings. The demonstrations died down but by then the force had undergone its bombing expansion and something had to be done wth the extra officers.

Administration Committee Chairman Wayne Hays, who pretty well can command almost as much service as the president of the United States, stationed three cops around-the-clock to guard an art exhibition he put together during the summer of 1973 in the offices of the Administration Committee. The paintings were done by some Hungarian refugee friends of Hays and while their work merited some praise no one except Hays seems ever to have heard of them. As it was, their scenes were better protected than priceless works a few blocks away at the National Gallery of Art.

You can also find cops standing outside the Rayburn and Longworth cafeterias, making sure that tourists and other members of the general public don't come in for lunch until the bulk of the staff has eaten.

And during the early days of the Senate Watergate hearings the *Washington Star-News* discovered Capitol police in plain clothes snapping pictures of the crowd in the Senate caucus room. The police explained that a picture would be handy in prosecuting someone who had disrupted the hearing. Handy yes, essential no; especially when hundreds of eyewitnesses were on hand.

It wouldn't be fair to conclude the visual appraisal without a few kind words about the Capitol police. For the most part, the man on the force (there are only two women on the organization, both of them Metropolitan District of Columbia officers detailed to the Capitol) is competent, hardworking and honest. In recent years, Congress has gradually transformed the force from one manned largely by political appointees to one made up primarily of retired and ex-military policemen. The new men tended at first to be a bit too efficient and humorless in their dealings with tourists (compared with the friendly and easygoing approach favored by the students whom they succeeded), but they have begun to relax and they do add a certain air of professionalism that did not exist in the past. Chief James M. Powell, a pleasant, patient man who has headed the Capitol police since 1965, is generally credited with doing a good job under difficult circumstances, not the least of which is the belief of many members of Congress that they have an inalienable right to run the force.

Statistical—As of 1974 the force had an authorized strength of 1,034—985 Capitol police plus 49 D.C. officers, such as Chief Powell, who are assigned or detailed to Congress and paid by Congress. With some 16,000 noncops working for the House and Senate, that produces a ratio of one protector to every sixteen persons protected. The District of Columbia, which has one of the lowest police-citizen ratios of any big city in the country, employs 5,000 officers for a population of 750,000, or one for every 160 persons. New York City's 30,000 policemen try to maintain law and order in a population of 8 million, which works out to one officer for every 266 residents.

Congress' police force patrols the Capitol, the five House and Senate office buildings, the old Congressional Hotel taken over by Congress a few years ago and the 155 acres of lawns, sidewalks, streets and roadways which by law comprise the Capitol grounds. To get around the area the police are equipped with 6 patrol cars, 18 motorbikes, and 2 surplus government buses used to transport contingents to a disturbance. The force also boasts a K-9 corps of 12 officers and 13 German shepherds, of which the latter group was expected to cost the government $4,000 to feed in 1974.

So that they can maintain efficient contact with each other, the police operate a communication system which features three radio channels and a capability for tape recording transmissions. The Capitol police are plugged into the Washington Area Law Enforcement System (WALES) and the FBI's National Crime Information Center, both of which transmit back to patrol cars computerized data on outstanding arrest warrants.

Much of the growth on Capitol Hill stands for something besides frills. It represents a congressional response to congressionally created conditions, i.e., new programs that create additional casework. But there are less defensible explanations. One of them is that the money is spent because, like the mountain, it is there.

The House is a private club, a club with a treasury that is virtually bottomless. It is a club which isn't about to be outdone in splendor by other clubs, like the Senate and the executive branch. So it will build, decorate, buy and pay for services without restraint.

Interestingly, few members will publicly or privately complain about the excessive and expensive examples of self-indulgence that they witness in the House. That goes for the liberals who consider themselves antiestablishment and the conservatives who consider themselves advocates of economy in government. Parsimonious H.R. Gross was one of the few lawmakers who had the courage and tenacity to raise hell over it. Although his flaying of colleagues was often justified it was rarely productive.

A year after it was completed, Gross was still furious about the redecoration of the Speaker's Lobby, carried out with little warning during the Easter recess of 1972. "I hesitate to contemplate the Easter recess coming up because the last time we left town for a period of time the members know what happened," he told the House.

It didn't take much self-indulging to infuriate Gross, who sustains his small, bony frame on the like of an American cheese sandwich and a glass of milk. His rage was compounded when he learned that his constituents' taxes were spent on ornate, "Louis the Fourteenth or Fifteenth or whatever" furnishings.

"We got chandeliers, beautiful crystal chandeliers!" he declared, with still lingering disbelief. "A $30,000 to $35,000 carpet and a complete outfit of new furniture, all at a cost of nearly $164,000!

"I hesitate to leave because I am afraid of what I will find when I return. The deeper the country goes into debt the plusher the surroundings in this place."

No such pain afflicts Wayne Hays, an unembarrassed spender of public moneys who about the same time that he was cooperating in redecorating the Speaker's Lobby was refurnishing his own Administration Committee offices with better taste, unmatched splendor and at an undisclosed cost. Hays enjoys needling Gross, and he met the Iowan's larger objection that day—his unhappiness with the proposed west front extension of the Capitol—by pointing out that the National Zoo had just spent $550,000 to house the two pandas given to the United States during President Nixon's visit to China.

"As far as the west wall is concerned," according to Hay's tabulation, "if we spend as much per member to do the west wall as they have spent per panda in the executive branch, we could build twice as much west front as we plan to build. . . ."

ℳ

Not only are there a lot of congressional employees, but considering salaries paid for similar work outside, especially in Washington, service in the cause of Congress can be rewarding. Except for a handful of officials, maximum employee pay on the Hill is $36,000 a year, due to go up a few thousand as soon as Congress musters the courage to raise its own pay above the present $42,500. Some top flight people making $36,000 could reap considerably more if they went into private industry. At the other end of the spectrum are people who perform no useful task whatsoever, either because their position should not exist in the first place or because they personally bring nothing but ineptitude to the job. The only impact that their departure would have on government operations would be a saving to the taxpayer of $36,000 a year. In between there are men and women who function at necessary jobs in undistinguished fashion, some overpaid, some underpaid and a plurality paid about what they merit.

At this point it would be well to take a moment to destroy the myth that working for the government earns you security but not much money. That was true at one time and may largely be true if you're a blue collar worker. But if you're a white collar employee of the federal government you stand an excellent chance of making more money than your counterpart in the private sector. (Ironically, what with the drastic and sporadic budget cutting and resulting agency layoffs of recent years, on-job security has lessened, especially for those without the seniority to bump someone under them into unemployment.) During the 1960s, federal employee unions and their allies in Congress pushed the theme of "comparability": in the interests of developing a classier civil service, and in fairness to public servants salaries should be raised to a level comparable to that of similar jobs on the outside. By 1970, following numerous congressionally ordered pay hikes, the civil servant had not only achieved comparability with his opposite in the private sector, he had in many areas surpassed him. Government statistics may claim otherwise, but many corporation executives maintain they are now having a hard time competing with government in recruiting secretaries, junior executives and professionals.

And if life has become sweet for the executive branch employee it has become even sweeter for average congressional white collar workers. Handsome salaries abound at the highest and lowest levels of responsibility.

In 1974, the clerk of the House received $40,000 a year and a chauffered limousine. Sixteen-year-old pages earned $7,864 in a year that usually included three months vacation. The House postmaster, at $31,500, got as much money as the postmaster of a major city. Former House Parliamentarian Lewis Deschler's paycheck was larger than that of the members he serves—$42,191 in salary and another $2,000 to compile the House precedents, a seemingly endless task that had been in progress for years.

Former doorkeeper William (Fishbait) Miller's administrative responsibilities and talents don't come near matching the national prominence he has achieved through his ceremonial chore of introducing presidents and other personages at joint sessions. Nevertheless, Miller pulled in $40,000. Sergeant at Arms Kenneth Harding has many more worries than Miller, including running the House bank and sharing in supervision of the police. He also has considerably more ability. Still, one might wonder whether the post justifies a salary of $40,000, considering that Washington's chief of police made only $36,000.

One of the best indicators of the congressional pay system's generosity can be found in the salaries received by experienced secretaries. No doubt these Hill secretaries are good, usually better informed, more responsive on the phone and given greater responsibility than their counterparts in the executive branch. At the same time they work long, hard hours, and without the overtime pay and job security offered by the government. But congressional secretaries more often than not are well-compensated for these sacrifices. In 1973 there were five secretaries on the House Armed Services Committee who made more than $21,000 a year. And virtually every committee plus many members' offices list one or more secretaries earning that kind of money. Add to this a few fringe benefits that are not available to downtown secretaries, such as free parking, cut-rate items from the House stationery store and an atmosphere of informality that permits occasional lively office parties. Yet in most cases Hill secretaries at least put in a solid day's labor for the handsome wages they receive. A multitude of men who work in the House do little more than fill a seat and grace a desk. Vegetating with a moribund subcommittee, hanging on with a generous or a somnolent member, they grab every raise that comes their way. They well might be making $36,000 a year in a job that literally could be eliminated without any adverse effect whatsoever on the public welfare.

Congress's spending on itself not only seems out of proportion with what's going on outside, it often doesn't make sense within its own borders. Disordered priorities pop up everywhere. For example, it's hard to reconcile how the House Internal Security Committee could spend almost

$1.4 million during the Ninety-second Congress while the Armed Services Committee spent only $381,028 during the same period. Leaving aside any ideological biases, the comparison is ludicrous. Armed Services, with a staff of about thirty, tackled a mountain of legislation, including some of the most important bills before Congress. It held hundreds of committee and subcommittee hearings, conducted lengthy investigations of defense activities, furnished an abundance of information to the House, maintained daily and voluminous contact with the Pentagon and answered thousands of letters from the public, ranging from criticisms of its actions to pleas for help from mistreated servicemen. Not all of us were happy with the product of those labors but we have to acknowledge that the committee worked its tail off.

The House Internal Security Committee, on the other hand, has achieved a legislative record of nonproduction that is legendary. Its latest chairman, Richard Ichord of Missouri, attempted to bring new respectability to the old Un-American Activities Committee by changing its name and by anchoring its investigative forays to some reasonably legitimate legislative purpose. While the committee's image was softened, its necessity hasn't increased one iota. In simple, cold fact, it could disappear tomorrow without leaving a ripple on the congressional pond. Attempts to sharply cut the committee's budget or abolish it altogether have failed because the vote on any such proposal quickly breaks down to an ideological litmus test that frightens middle-of-the-road congressmen. Ironically, the committee over the past decade has supplied its conservative adherents with little of substance and they would do well to tally up the millions the committee's scampering has cost their economy-minded constituents.

Inconsistencies show up elsewhere. Some of the congressional employees running the press galleries often receive more money than the newsmen they are serving. That probably says something about the economic equity of the news business but it also says something about congressional salaries. Jerry Landauer, in a 1972 *Wall Street Journal* article on Hill pay, noted that in return for greeting visitors and answering the phone ex-Congressman William Springer's secretary was making nearly three times as much money as the average American factory worker. And roughly one-third of all American families, Landauer observed, lived on less than Congress paid its adolescent pages for running errands.

The supply of money for staff needs is not endless— quite. By 1974 members were limited to a lump sum annual staff allowance of $194,004, from which they could employ no more than sixteen persons at a time. The maximum salary they could pay any one person was $33,710 a year. Committee funding, however, was far more liberal. Theoretically, a committee could spend as much on salaries as the House authorized it to draw from the annual legislative appropriation. Chairmen present their budgets to the Administration Committee and unless it's outrageously out of line or tied up in a personality dispute, which doesn't happen often, the Administration Committee O.K.s the proposal and sends it along to the House floor for routine approval. If the committee sees its work load increasing, it need only ask for more money. The only limitation facing it is the maximum it can pay an employee, which in 1974 was $36,000 and ready to burst to new heights as soon as Congress cleared the way for a boost in its own pay. Members with seniority, such as Springer, who before his retirement was ranking Republican on the Commerce Committee, are able to utilize the committee staff they are entitled to and employ him or her in their own offices. Thus Springer's receptionist was technically a staff member of the Commerce Committee.

Along the same lines, but in grosser and in clearly illegal fashion, some members are able to place on their staffs political associates who perform no official services for the public. The late Charles Buckley, a machine boss in the Bronx and chairman of the Public Works Committee in Washington, broke all records when he doled out fifteen jobs from his committee and congressional staffs to political lieutenants back home in New York. *Washington Star* reporter Paul Hope drew blank stares and "no comments" in 1964 when he asked Buckley's cohorts what they did for the more than $100,000 a year they were collectively collecting. Buckley said what they did was "my business."

"I know what they're doing. They go where I tell them and do what I tell them," declared Buckley. The taxpayers rebounded that year when reformer Jonathan Bingham upset Buckley in the Democratic primary and knocked the old war horse and his friends off the government payroll.

6

A Tale of Two Congressmen

F. EDWARD HÉBERT and Benjamin S. Rosenthal are both Democrats. One other fact links the two congressmen. Louis Armstrong was born in Hébert's hometown of New Orleans and died in the Elmhurst-Corona section of Queens in New York, which is where Rosenthal is from. On the surface, that's pretty much where the similarities end.

Hébert is the prototype of a vanishing breed, the southern conservative Democrat who is powerful, as in "the powerful chairman of the House Armed Services Committee," which he has been since 1971. He is also powerful because he has been in Congress since 1941 and has squeezed out every perquisite and prerogative due him by virtue of his seniority. In 1974 it could be said that Hébert was the Last of the Titans. He was unbending in his rightist ideology, shrewd in combat, flamboyant in style and comfortable with power. Other men in the House of Representatives still had these traits, but Hébert was the only one who possessed all of them.

Rosenthal is not flamboyant. He is extremely interesting,

but you have to listen to him for awhile to find that out. He came to Congress in 1962, so after twelve years, which isn't very long by House longevity standards, he doesn't have much power. And he may or may not stay around until he does. He is liberal and while Hébert believes it will always be politically and morally safe to stick with the old-fashioned verities, Rosenthal does a lot of thinking and questioning and worrying and criticizing, and gets a lot of flak in return. He is what has come to be known as an issue-oriented legislator.

Neither man could be called an average representative but both do personify opposite and extreme poles of political style and philosophy, poles which are regarded as benchmarks by colleagues in the great middle ground, those members who more frequently shift with the currents of public opinion and the issues of the day.

You could do worse than follow around Hébert and Rosenthal to get a feel for the House.

F. EDWARD HÉBERT

The late L. Mendel Rivers holds the all-time won-and-lost record for chairman of the House Services Committee. Rivers never lost a bill in committee or on the floor, an accomplishment, he noted one day, that even "Caesar in all his glory" couldn't equal.

Because he came to power during a time when the military's hold over the House was beginning to wane, F. Edward Hébert's record as chairman wasn't quite as good as Rivers's. It was good, all right, but Hébert lost now and then. What Hébert had over Rivers, however, was knowing how to enjoy the job. Rivers brooded a lot, stormed around, chewed out people and generally took himself and his responsibilities very seriously. Hébert, on the other hand, viewed his legislative and political struggles as a sport. Ideology was important, of course, but the fun came in playing the game and winning.

Another reason Hébert enjoyed being chairman and congressman so much was that a lot of people were always doing things for him. Some of the people were powerful, like the president of the United States and members of his cabinet. Others who still cater to him include fellow congressmen, staff aides, military officers, defense contractors, his wife, two chauffeurs and a passel of people back in New Orleans who have been boosting him since he was city editor at the New Orleans *States* in the 1930s.

It is early spring, 1973. The phone rings; Hébert picks it up. Navy Secretary John Warner is returning the chairman's call. Some brief joshing follows. Then Hébert gets to the point.

"Listen, John, I just had some Navy League people here from New Orleans. They're planning a big affair for next Navy Day. Could you come down and be their speaker? It's October twelfth."

It was doubtful whether Warner even checked his calendar. In a split second, Hébert was closing the conversation with warm thanks.

It's fair to say that any of the armed forces' secretaries would have responded as quickly and positively. But in the continuing service rivalry of who can do more for Chairman Hébert, the navy has been winning hands down.

The navy wrapped up the championship when it relocated its reserve headquarters, as well as the headquarters for the marines, in New Orleans. A few other facilities were tossed in and before anyone but Hébert realized it, metropolitan New Orleans faced the happy prospect of housing a sprawling new defense complex, which by 1977 was expected to generate an annual payroll of $100 million.

The navy, which had already loaded down Rivers's hometown of Charleston, South Carolina, with just about all that it could handle, went after Hébert on a more personal and direct level at the same time it was sending all that military pork barrel his way. At one point, it dispatched a hotshot pilot to Capitol Hill to serve as Hébert's personal liaison officer. The young commander was enthusiastic and inventive. For example, after Hébert landed Secretary Warner as the Navy Day speaker in New Orleans, the officer quickly lined up 500 naval cadets and the Navy Fife and Drum Corps to accompany the secretary. Hébert took a fatherly liking to the commander but finally induced the navy to call him off, pointing out that he couldn't think of things to keep him busy. Besides, the other services, as well as the navy's regular congressional liaison office, were getting envious. Actually, Hébert had broken in the navy well before he became chairman. A few years prior he "persuaded" the Naval Academy to abandon its policy of playing no postseason football games and booked them for the Sugar Bowl in New Orleans. Similarly, he helped out colleague Tip O'Neill and convinced a reluctant academy that it ought to play the opening game at the new stadium of Boston College, O'Neill's alma mater.

In his own way, former President Nixon was as attentive to Hébert's personal and political needs as the services. Nixon salved the Hébert ego with in-flight phone calls from Air Force One and by showing up at functions in Washington honoring Hébert—such as the Tulane Appreciation Dinner in May, 1971, and, a few months later, the hanging of the new chairman's portrait in the Armed Services Committee's hearing room.

More significantly, Nixon delivered on matters of substance. For years, Hébert had been pushing a pet project—the establishment of a military medical school, a multimillion dollar institution to turn out doctors for the services. All this time the idea lay dormant, viewed as another military boondoggle by liberals and as intrusion into what had always been a private sector responsibility by the conservatives. In the Nixon administration just about every department in government except the Pentagon opposed it. The Office of Management and Budget added its crucial vote of disapproval. Outside of government the American Medical Association and all of its state branches except the one in Louisiana registered their objections. In 1972, Armed Services Committee Chairman Hébert got Congress to approve the necessary legislation and Nixon signed it—in the very year that he waged a ruthless antispending campaign in Washington.

The object of all this attention is known to his friends and admirers as "Eddie." To his detractors, it's Hébert. Nobody calls him Edward, nor Felix, which is what the "F" stands for. The last name receives the full French pronunciation (Ay'-behr) and, although he can spin off Cajun phrases, he admits he can't speak French. What he does speak is English in a strong, hoarse voice with a thick, unpretentious New Orleans accent. It comes out sounding like a southerner trying to speak Brooklynese, as in "Tell 'em I'll probably fly down *cuhmoicial* and to meet me at the *ehpoht.*" He likes to kid and he likes to pass on confidences. He'll do both in a booming stage whisper, usually grabbing the lapel of a hapless listener.

Physically, he looms large but not overpowering. His broad face is distinguished by a wide thin mouth, a long full nose, receding white hair and dark horn-rimmed glasses with thick lenses. One eye was blinded by a childhood accident; the other came perilously close to succumbing to a cataract. It is not a gentle face but neither is it menacing. Nor is it as tough as it was in the thirties. Old photographs show a dark, sometimes scowling countenance glaring from under a broadbrimmed fedora. When he was fifty and his hair was black, Hébert looked surprisingly like Lyndon Johnson looked as president.

Historically, his most celebrated namesake was Jacques Hébert, the radical journalist who helped inflame and then was devoured by the French Revolution. Today's Hébert says he doesn't know if he's related to the Jacobinite Hébert and professes not to care. It may be that he could do without additional identification with a card-carrying revolutionary. A few years ago he had the Library of Congress research another journalistic ancestor, this one a great-grandfather from Louisiana on his mother's side. He was a bit stunned at what the library found.

"The old son of a bitch was on the wrong side of every issue. They practically ran him out of the goddamn city. Like taking up for the blacks during Reconstruction days. After that I didn't want to know anything more about my ancestors." Yet there's a side of the nineteenth-century editor that appeals to his conservative descendant. After telling the story Hébert remarks in an uncharacteristic display of quiet admiration: "But he must have been a man of great courage, to stand up for those things."

Interestingly, it was a swashbuckling newspaper career which propelled Hébert into politics, a career which included stints as a sportswriter, press agent (at times simultaneously), political columnist and finally as city editor at the *States*. It was in this last job that he hit paydirt with an investigative series exposing what came to be known in the state as the Louisiana Scandals, a saga of official corruption which sent remnants of the Long machine to prison —and Hébert to Washington. The journalistic muscle flexing inspired him to take a crack at the ten-year incumbent congressman. He knocked him off in the primary by a two-to-one vote and at the age of thirty-nine took his seat in the House as representative of Louisiana's First Congressional District.

Thirty years later, at the age of sixty-nine, he reached another pinnacle of success, chairmanship of the Armed Services Committee. But the long wait was neither unpleasant nor uneventful. It included a relatively brief but historic tour with the House Un-American Activities Committee (HUAC), one in which he turned his free swinging investigative style to work nailing Alger Hiss and joining the great hunt for communists in government. One of his fellow HUAC members was freshman Republican Rep. Richard Nixon and the smooth and warm relationship the two men established would survive for many years.

Harry Truman and his attorney general, Tom Clark, thought precious little of the committee, and less of Democratic members like Hébert who fueled its forays during the Republican controlled Eightieth Congress. Hébert didn't improve his standing with the White House when he bolted the Truman-Barkley ticket in 1948 and backed Strom Thurmond's States's Rights bid for the presidency. After the election in January, 1949, the House Democratic leadership bounced him off the Un-American Activities Committee. It accomplished the purge by persuading the Democratic caucus to require that Democratic members of HUAC be lawyers, thereby neatly eliminating newspaperman Hébert while preserving the integrity of the sacred seniority system.

That experience shaped the attitude that Hébert would

adopt toward the national party for the rest of his political career: pay no attention to it but keep your mouth shut and take it for what you can get, i.e., the fruits of congressional seniority. If the party's candidates or positions were too much for a southern conservative to stomach, then the southern conservative would maintain a public silence while privately reminding constituents it was in New Orlean's interest every now and then to swallow a bit of pride. Discretion became part of his political arsenal. He still voiced his old tenets, but he carefully refrained from saying or doing anything that would give mainline Democrats an opportunity to bounce him off the Armed Services Committee as they had bounced him off HUAC.

The increasing years of service earned him subcommittee chairmanships, positions of power from which he conducted peppery probes into military ineptitude or dishonesty. Nothing he uncovered, however, disturbed the boyhood conviction that won him a debating contest at Jesuit High School: "Shall we be defenseless America, a weak and harmless nation, or shall we be defensive America, the fear and dread of all nations?"

Hébert's congressional career did produce one major change, tilting him away from a life dominated by conflict and enriched by pleasure to one which reversed the dosage. Now there was time and occasion to amass the creature comforts that were available to him through privilege and his own money, the accumulation of which he attributes to some early New Orleans real estate deals that turned "two one-hundred dollar bills into $100,000."

In Washington he delighted in maintaining the Bourbon Street image—the lover of good food and drink, clothes that occasionally bordered on the outrageous (like a seersucker suit with a vest) and a suburban home in Alexandria, Virginia, which with the addition of white columns and a weeping willow tree he transformed into an antebellum mansion. And somehow he managed to latch on to the largest and most uniquely configured office suite in the Rayburn Building. It came complete with a spacious entrance alcove, which he graced with a birdbath.

The style, the personality, the good-natured cynicism made him popular in the House. For those who didn't share his ideology he was at least an adversary who didn't seem to take himself or the issues all that seriously. He was someone who kidded and could take kidding in return. During a floor debate, Otis Pike could liken him to a Mississippi riverboat gambler, knowing that Hébert would delight in the characterization. Reporters enjoyed him for many of the same reasons and because he was accessible and quotable. When they didn't call he would drop in on the press gallery to kibitz.

That is one side of Eddie Hébert. The other side, seen less often in Washington, is that of a man with a stern sense of retribution and an ultraconservative political philosophy. His response to the dark and angry days of the late 1960s brought out that less amiable side of his character.

When Dr. Martin Luther King, Jr., was assassinated Hébert issued a statement deploring murder. But he contended that King had preached violence under the guise of nonviolence and that violence followed in his wake. In an attempt to prove that King "aroused people to violence," Hébert triumphantly noted in reply to one angry letter writer that King closed one of his most memorable speeches with the lines, "Mine eyes have seen the glory of the coming of the Lord."

"This sentence is taken from the 'Battle Hymn of the Republic' which was the fighting song of the Northern troops during the Civil War. If this is not arousing to violence, I do not know what is," Hébert declared.

Robert Kennedy's assassination two months later was linked to the decline of law and order in the country, a condition which Hébert blamed on the Supreme Court and the Justice Department's refusal to "enforce the laws which are on the books."

The previous year Hébert conducted hearings on the use of National Guard troops in the Detroit riots. He led the yahoo brigade in denouncing the administration for what members felt was its soft handling of looters and arsonists. Particularly galling to them was the order, handed down shortly after the Michigan guard was federalized, that guardsmen were to unload their rifles and were not to reload or fire them without specific permission from an officer. The congressmen were convinced the directive had emanated from civilian do-gooders in the Pentagon, Justice Department or White House. They would have perpetuated the myth had it not been for the forthright testimony of Lt. Gen. John L. Throckmorton, the beribboned regular army officer who commanded the operation. He accepted full responsibility for issuing the order.

"If I had to do it again, I would do it exactly the same way," he testified. "I was confronted with a group of trigger-happy, nervous soldiers in the National Guard. I had no intention of having any of those soldiers shoot innocent people or small children."

In New Orleans he was the fighting city editor-turned-battling congressman. Instead of the Long machine, he was taking on President Harry Truman and his attorney general, Tom Clark, over the Un-American Activities Committee. Years later he resisted and sometimes blocked Robert McNamara's efforts to lop off some of the more nonsensical features of the Defense Department and to exercise a greater degree of civilian control over the place.

Hébert made sure the press back home knew what he was doing and played it the way he wanted.

For a long time, friends from the New Orleans media establishment treated with reverence the unabashedly self-serving press releases he churned out of his office. A few years ago there was a break in the ranks. It involved only one newspaper, but it happened to be the successor to Hébert's old paper, the New Orleans *States-Item*. Hébert never forgave it for its drift toward liberalism or its criticism of him and his positions. At the slightest conversational opening, he would venomously denounce it. In the fall of 1972 the *States-Item*'s editors confirmed his suspicion that they had taken leave of their senses and patriotic obligations. The *States-Item* endorsed George McGovern for president, one of the few newspapers in the South—or for that matter, in the nation—to do so.

During the long years that Carl Vinson ran the Armed Services Committee, Hébert was one of several senior subcommittee chairmen. When Vinson retired in 1965 and turned over the committee to Mendel Rivers, Hébert became the new chairman's confidant, counselor and first choice to handle the most important investigations. Hébert went after the Pentagon, but usually his targets were the civilian chiefs, whom he accused of muzzling the generals and admirals or of weakening America's military strength.

His most delicate assignment was the investigation of the My Lai massacre. Although Rivers was hoping the army could be exonerated, and his own sympathies were such that he could not have enjoyed the task, Hébert conducted a thorough probe of the affair. While the subcommittee's report contained its weaknesses and omissions, by no stretch of the imagination could it have been called the white-wash that many had predicted.

An equally demanding task facing Hébert was keeping the reins on Rivers. He constantly urged moderation on his friend and, if that seems incredible in light of Rivers's headline-making outbursts, the fact is that without Hébert there would have been more outrageous proclamations than there were.

When Rivers returned to the House after a ten-day drying-out session at Bethesda Naval Hospital—one of the few occasions he went off the wagon after becoming chairman—he was greeted by a devastating Drew Pearson column vividly recounting the details of what had been a closely guarded secret. Rivers's first impulse was to take the floor and lash out at Pearson. But Hébert persuaded him that a direct counterattack would simply spread the story well beyond Pearson's readership. He prevailed upon Rivers to hold his fire and let him take care of it. He did, arranging for members of the House establishment to welcome Mendel back from his "illness" through a round of tributes delivered at the start of a debate Rivers was managing. Not a mention was made of the Pearson column, leaving reporters hard pressed to recirculate the charges but filled to the brim with reams of praisemaking quotes about Rivers.

On December 28, 1970, Mendel Rivers died of a heart ailment. The next senior Democrat, Philip Philbin, had lost reelection to Father Robert Drinan in the Massachusetts Democratic primary and would not be back when the Ninety-second Congress convened in January, 1971. Thus, in his seventieth year, F. Edward Hébert became chairman of the House Armed Services Committee.

Things went swimmingly for the first two years of his chairmanship. Hébert kept up Rivers's perfect won-and-lost record on the bills he brought to the floor and, by doing so, maintained the House's solid promilitary stance. And he racked up the legislative accomplishments without generating the enemies that Rivers had.

On the floor and in committee Hébert managed to avoid the antagonism that Rivers had so often created for himself by trying to ride roughshod over opponents. Rivers had triggered angry outbursts on several occasions when he arbitrarily decided that there had been enough talk on a bill or amendment and rallied a majority to cut off further debate. Hébert, on the other hand, figured no harm would be done by allowing the opposition to talk itself out. In the end, like Rivers, he invariably won anyhow. But unlike his predecessor he was able to walk off the floor listening to adversaries acclaiming his fairness.

At the same time, Hébert renewed his old friendship with Nixon, and soon the two had established a working relationship that benefited both. Hébert bailed out Nixon on Vietnam, twice in 1971 supplying instrumental aid in blocking House acceptance of the Senate-passed Mansfield antiwar amendment. When Nixon undertook his momentous initiatives toward China and Russia Hébert protected his right flank by seeing to it that no criticism was heard from the conservative councils of the Armed Services Committee.

In return, Nixon took care of Hébert and New Orleans. Ego-massaging started almost immediately. Matters of substance followed. Hébert got his military medical school, an idea that Democratic and Republican administrations had been rejecting as impractical and unnecessary since 1947. The military began paying more attention to the New Orleans area, upgrading facilities there and considering what more might fit. The navy found the choicest plum, announcing in 1973 it was consolidating headquarters for all of its and the Marine Corps Reserve programs. The new location—New Orleans. Other support activities were also ordered switched to New Orleans. For the city, it represented a gift package that included $40 million worth of renovation and related expenditures, a $35 million-a-year payroll and guaranteed immortality for Hébert. Sen. Carl Curtis of Nebraska charged that the whole operation was a "rotten mess" and that the navy engineered it in order to "cater to the demands and wishes" of Hébert. Although Curtis stood as a paragon of loyal Republicanism, Nixon ignored him and went on catering to Democrat Hébert.

At the beginning of 1973, with two years under his belt as a committee chairman, Hébert looked forward to continued success. True, the Democratic caucus had recently adopted rules intended to diminish the power of committee chairmen. But Hébert had artfully finessed his way around them when the Armed Services Committee organized itself for the start of the Ninety-third Congress.

"I've got more power now than Carl Vinson had in fifty years," he boasted to a visitor in early March.

Soon, however, Hébert's world began to sour a bit. Support in the House for the military and the administration's Indochina policy was slipping drastically. No longer was there automatic reverence for the judgments of the Armed Services Committee. Noisy, junior liberals had joined the panel and were snipping away at the chairman, or more often, the weapons programs he was pushing. The liberals in themselves weren't a serious threat. The committee was still overwhelmingly behind Hébert on almost all issues. But they annoyed Hébert and prodded him into counterattacking. It was a new and unsettling experience. For years he had done the attacking—going after Harry Truman and his attorney general, Tom Clark; years later Clark's son, Ramsey, Robert McNamara and the "Whiz

Kids" who worked for the defense secretary. If Hébert wasn't the original target, he at least found himself spending a lot of time defending his own and others' policies and actions. It was getting to him. Hints of yearning for the old days appeared.

Les Aspin, one of those on Hébert's list of annoyances, was on the House floor one day when, to his surprise, Hébert sat down next to him and opened up a conversation.

"He said, 'You know it's great being a junior member on the committee. You can do almost anything you damn please, take any stance you want, be as irresponsible as you want. You can really have a lot of fun.' I think what he was trying to say was that senior members on any committee have to play pretty much around the center and they have different types of problems."

When Democratic liberal Patricia Schroeder joined his committee in 1973, Hébert joshed to the press that the pretty thirty-two-year-old freshman would serve as the panel's "den mother." The cheerful Mrs. Schroeder went along and said she was sure she and Hébert would hit it off fine despite their ideological differences. That was in the winter of 1973. Three months later they were at each other's throats.

The collapse of good will started over small matters. When the air force invited members of the committee to a tour of bases, Mrs. Schroeder asked Hébert why he was permitting the military to finance a congressional junket, suggesting that the arrangement might undermine the committee's objectivity.

"That's ridiculous," exploded Hébert. "What the hell difference does it make where the money comes from. It's all out of the same budget."

Mrs. Schroeder set off Hébert again when she wrote a

minority opinion to the committee's annual weapons procurement bill, urging a cutback in the navy's aircraft carrier force.

"What the hell does she know about carriers," Hébert
grumbled to a visitor.

By spring Hébert was describing Mrs. Schroeder as a
"scatterbrain . . . a real pain in the ass." She was describing
him as "vicious . . . a true autocrat.

"Anything that's said against him, he zeroes in on you
and threatens you with all sorts of things. That's how he
operates and I think it's totally unfair."

No more jokes about den mothers. "We're at war now,"
she disclosed. "It's terrible, it's no longer funny."

That was said in May, 1973. In July their war was to
escalate still further. Speaker Albert designated Mrs.
Schroeder as one of thirteen House members to serve as
congressional advisor to the U.S. delegation at an upcoming disarmament conference in Geneva. State Department
red tape required that Mrs. Schroeder get an authorization
from the chairman of her committee. Figuring that his consent would be perfunctory, she wrote Hébert asking him to
notify the State Department that she would be traveling on
official committee business. To Hébert it wasn't perfunctory at all, but rather an opportunity to get back at Mrs.
Schroeder for her complaints about Pentagon-sponsored
junkets.

"I am unaware of my having designated you to represent
the Committee on Armed Services for this purpose," he
wrote back. "Therefore, I regret that I am unable to send
the letter you request."

Mrs. Schroeder was furious. She learned that another
junior member, Bill Alexander of Arkansas, was running
into similar difficulties with the Government Operations
Committee. The two went to Albert and said they weren't

going to put up with it. Albert prevailed upon them to hold tight while he worked things out. The Speaker came through and confrontations were avoided. Had he not, Mrs. Schroeder had a letter ready which she was prepared to send to Hébert and which she supposedly summarized to him verbally.

In it she said she was "astonished' at his refusal to authorize her trip and reminded him that he had invited her to represent the committee at such functions as the Paris Air Show. She had learned, she added, that his action was prompted by her committee voting record and "my temerity" in filing dissenting views on the carrier issue.

"I believe, Mr. Chairman, that the day has passed when the power of a position such as you hold can be used to compel uniformity of vote or view. Members of Congress are responsible to their constituents and to their consciences—not to their committee chairman."

Another new member who got to Hébert that year was Ronald Dellums, the black second-termer from Berkeley, California, who in his first term established an antiwar, antimilitary record that satisfied his constituency but which marked him as a veritable bomb-thrower in the eyes of Hébert and his compatriots. In 1973 Dellums switched over to Armed Services from the Foreign Affairs Committee after the Democratic leadership cleared the way for the transfer. Hébert never forgave Speaker Albert or Wilbur Mills, chairman of the Democrats' Committee on Committees, for yielding to pressure from the Congressional Black Caucus, which had engineered the move.

(Hébert apparently had been harboring a grudge against Mills for years. During a conversation with me in 1973, he alluded to dusty suspicions that Mills may have been the creator of the "no-lawyer" rule which forced him off HUAC. "I never could trust the son of a bitch," he muttered. "I've known him for thirty years and never trusted him.")

Hébert insisted that his opposition to Dellums was based on Dellums's radical politics and rhetoric, not his race.

"He came to see me on the floor and said he wanted to get on the committee. I told him I wasn't against him because he was black. 'I'm color blind,' I told him. I don't care whether he's black or white. I want Americans on the committee. I said if he could get on through the regular rules, I won't object. He said that was fair enough for him and we shook hands."

That era of understanding lasted about as long as the peace pact with Patricia Schroeder. Tensions that were building up between the old southern conservative warhorse and the mod black leftist exploded on May 1, 1973.

The committee was behind closed doors questioning Admiral Elmo Zumwalt, Chief of Naval Operations, about the navy's requests for the coming year. Committee counsel Frank Slatinshek had just confronted Zumwalt with a committee staff study critical of the readiness of navy ships. Slatinshek noted that many congressmen on the committee felt the poor record could be traced to "inadequate discipline and inadequate leadership on these ships," a thinly veiled allusion to Zumwalt's publicized efforts at modernizing the navy's social attitudes—through such steps as permitting men to grow beards—and improving race relations.

Slatinshek's implication infuriated Zumwalt.

"I find it absolutely amazing to hear a statement like that, Mr. Slatinshek . . . I think your comment is a disgrace to the U.S. Navy."

Dellums, who appreciated what Zumwalt and others in the military were trying to do for black servicemen, didn't like the thrust of the staff study either. And he especially didn't appreciate the fact that he didn't know such a report existed.

Dellums objected that committee members had not seen the study. Hébert gave the objection short shrift, telling Dellums that no one had ever complained about the way the committee conducted its business until Dellums joined it. Back came Dellums. Back came Hébert. Voices rose. Finally, in an attempt to separate the two, another member interrupted with a question for Zumwalt. But the break was short-lived, more like a referee pulling apart two fighters in a clinch. Hébert moved in again.

"It would be of interest to the members of the committee to know that the gentleman from California arrived the other day in Mr. Slatinshck's office with a lawyer and a staff member, to see secret documents. God, I have been on this committee thirty-two years and I have never heard of that happening before."

Hébert then moved in for the kill.

"I will not indict anybody or impugn anybody, but I have my own opinion of these tactics. . . . The situation is closed. All I will say to the gentleman is, he is on this committee. He got on the committee in an unusual manner. He got on the committee, and any day he doesn't like to serve on the committee, that door is open."

Dellums wasn't about to let it end there.

"I am going to serve on this committee for at least two years, Mr. Chairman, whether you like it or not." And he did. But that was to be only one source of irritation for Hébert.

On July 31, 1973, for the first time in memory, the House overrode the recommendations of the Armed Services Committee and, on amendment by Aspin, cut a substantial chunk of money from the annual weapons procurement bill, slicing nearly $1 billion from the $21.4 billion measure. Hébert eventually recouped most of the money through some fast card shuffling in the conference with Senate Armed Services Committee members, but the damage to pride had been done.

It was the second time in three months that a majority of the House had rejected his counsel. On the first occasion they were downright rude. That heresy occurred on May 10, 1973, the day the House of Representatives cast its first vote ever against the war in Indochina. Hébert, rushing to the aid of the president and Appropriations Committee Chairman George Mahon, whose bill was under attack, tried desperately to prevent the House from turning dove. He took the floor in an attempt to spike the charge that the United States—despite the agreed-upon ceasefire in Vietnam four months earlier—was getting itself back into the war through its continued bombing of Cambodia and Laos. Members literally hooted Hébert.

A couple of months later I asked Hébert if the jeering had bothered him much. He shrugged it off, mumbling that it was just a handful of people and that it merely irritated rather than angered him. But he soon made it apparent that it had gotten to him more than he would admit.

"They're not logical. They don't listen."

He had reached the point of disgust where he didn't care anymore. Given the gloomy military outlook at the time, he was ready to end direct U.S. combat support in Cambodia.

"And when it goes down the drain and the domino theory takes place, then look around and see whose face is going to be red."

He was disappointed in the House, feeling that it was giving in just as events were justifying its years of hawkishness. Men such as himself and the late Mendel Rivers had long advocated letting the military "go in and get it over with." Now they finally had a president who had done just that and, in their view, had proven the United States could unleash its military might without setting off a world war.

"They threw their hands up in holy horror at the Christmas bombing . . . if the Christmas bombing hadn't taken place the prisoners of war would still be in Vietnam. That brought 'em to their knees."

We talked some more that day about the Vietnam War, and then about war in general. I asked him about the accusation of pacifists throughout history that it was old men who started wars for young men to fight. In Hébert's case, the point was more than theoretical. He was seventy-two years old now. Because of his age and partial blindness he had missed World War II. His only child was a female. The lack of personal involvement did not embarrass him. The reaction was immediate.

"Bullshit. Always the younger man has got to fight the war." He paused slightly, and then added, "For that I feel very sorry."

All around us were visible reminders of past sacrifices. Hébert's office walls were laden with citations and plaques of appreciation from the armed services, with crossed scabbards and captured communist weapons, with a massive Howard Chandler Christy painting of the Iwo Jima flag-raising and on the opposite wall, a sentimental portrait of two little girls praying for the return of their POW daddy from North Vietnam.

For a man who never served in the military, Hébert was surrounded by military men, military trappings, military events.

Besides the mementos and the other things in his Capitol office, besides the committee business which must be dealt with daily, Hébert spends most of the day talking to military officials, both uniformed and civilian.

He will not recoil at the charge that he is a friend of the military. He readily and proudly admits it. That does not, he always adds, include looking the other way when the military trips up. He says he has avoided taking any campaign contributions from defense contractors and has banned the committee staff from accepting any favors from industry representatives, even lunch.

In order to achieve a more thorough scrutiny of military spending requests, I asked him why it wouldn't be preferable for the committee to maintain an adversary relationship toward the Pentagon.

"To be objective you don't have to be an adversary. You don't have to be a bulldog tearing down everything. To make the system of checks and balances and separation of powers work you don't have to be on their ass all the time."

Hanging in the reception room of Hébert's Rayburn Building office are the signed photographs of American presidents dating back to Franklin Roosevelt. Except for one, all of them—including the four fellow Democrats who served in the office—carry perfunctory inscriptions, words that could apply to any congressman. Underneath the picture of Republican Richard Nixon is the handwritten note:

"To Congressman Edward Hébert, with appreciation for his years of splendid service to the nation and with the warmest personal regards from his friend. Dick Nixon."

Notwithstanding his claims of invulnerability to ego-massaging, it was apparent that the special, personal relationship which flowered between Hébert and the former president of the United States helped to make life bearable at a time when it seemed as if the old order was giving way to a new and troublesome era. Nixon wasn't the first president he had known but he was the first Hébert felt close to.

"Truman, I fought with tooth and nail. But I think he's one of the great presidents. The man had guts. Undoubtedly, the most talented was Roosevelt. I liked Jack Kennedy a lot. Eisenhower was a political general but he ran the White House like an army staff. I knew Johnson perhaps better than any of the others except Nixon. I'm fonder of Nixon than all of them. Ideologically, Nixon and I agree. All the other characters I disagreed with.

"When we were on the Un-American Activities Committee I discovered that his philosophy and mine were the same. I'm closer to him now since he is president and I am chairman than perhaps at any other time. And it's a very warm relationship. A very personal relationship."

Hébert stuck with Nixon to the end, maintaining even after Nixon resigned that it was those around him that had brought about the president's downfall.

Between presidential calls, Hébert is devotedly cared for by his wife, Gladys, and staff. Mrs. Hébert is a pleasant, slightly salty, imperturbable woman who years ago accepted the fact that she would have to adapt her life to her husband's high voltage existence. For eighteen years she worked in his office. After she quit she would often travel with him on his frequent trips between Washington and New Orleans. She seems to enjoy the political life and yet she appears to be able to keep it in perspective. She wisecracks, calls him "Hébert" in public and generally refuses to take too seriously all the folderol he finds his way into.

Hébert's personal staff is relatively small but gets the job done. Keeping the staff below the maximum size authorized allows Hébert to spread around the available allowance a bit more liberally. Mary Swann, his administrative assistant, received a salary in 1974 of $33,700. Virginea

Burguieres, who runs his New Orleans office, makes almost as much. So much for Hébert's vote against the Equal Rights Amendment.

An engaging, polite young man with the name of Lou Gehrig Burnett handles Hébert's press relations, a task fraught with pitfalls considering the congressman's conviction that he is still the best reporter/press agent in town. Nor is the job made easier by Hébert's penchant for occasionally refusing to deal with certain news organizations. But somehow Burnett manages to satisfy his boss and provide reporters with a striking amount of useful and frank information.

Hébert delegates to his receptionist, Alma Moore, almost complete authority to make his appointments. Like similar women on the Hill, she has an uncanny sense of knowing who her boss ought to see and demonstrates a talent for gently putting off those she knows he does not want to see.

Because of his eyesight impairment, Hébert cannot drive. He hired two chauffeurs—one for Washington, the other for New Orleans—and put them on his staff. He justifies paying them with government funds on the grounds that the money is at his disposal to be used as he sees fit.

Softening the discomfort of shuttling constantly between Washington and New Orleans are comfortable homes in Alexandria, Virginia, and New Orleans, as well as a lodge in New Iberia, Louisiana. I was to learn that in New Orleans life is even sweeter for Hébert than it is in the Capitol.

In the fall of 1972 I told Hébert I wanted to see how he operated in New Orleans and asked him to suggest an appropriate time. He proposed Navy Day, October 12, when the local Navy League chapter, a civilian organization that serves as a booster of both the navy and Hébert, would celebrate Navy Day and the congressman's seventy-first birthday.

I spent two days in New Orleans. I didn't learn much of how Hébert treated his constituents, but I learned how some of his constituents treated him. Grandly. Hébert promised me a good show, a promise he could keep because he helped arrange the show.

It included a two-day appearance by Marine Corps Commandant Robert E. Cushman, Jr., (the following year he collared Navy Secretary John Warner); a flight demonstration by two of the navy's new Harrier "short take-off and landing" aircraft; dedication of a new marine headquarters building (named after Hébert); a luncheon at Brennan's hosted by the F. Edward Hébert Chapter of the Marine Corps Reserve Association; dinner at Antoine's, hosted by the president of the Navy League Chapter; a parade through downtown New Orleans the next morning followed by a grand finale Navy League luncheon featuring "the beloved dean of the Louisiana Congressional Delegation," as he was described in the program, Cushman, a phalanx of color guards, a three-tiered head table and a mass, on-stage swearing-in of a score of navy recruits.

Although they were a bit beyond the ordinary, even by his standards, the two days I spent in New Orleans provided, I am told, a reasonably accurate portrayal of the kind of esteem in which Hébert is held by a segment of his district.

"It's news," said one New Orleans reporter, "when Hébert comes home and doesn't get a citation for patriotism."

It's hard to tell how seriously Hébert takes all the hoopla performed in his behalf. In Washington he is forever happily arranging events in New Orleans at which he is usually the honored guest or main speaker. Frequently the invitation is accompanied by a request that the congressman bring down a big name with him, such as a cabinet member or one of the Joint Chiefs. Hébert never fails to come through. Watching him put one of these affairs together is like witnessing a jovial toastmaster planning his own testimonial.

Over the years, Hébert has done a good deal of string pulling for his district. Even before he became chairman of the Armed Services Committee he was busy grabbing off excess federal land for local uses or keeping alive marginal federal activities which in other parts of the country already would have been shut down.

In the spring of 1974 Hébert proudly summed up his accomplishments with a press release. It noted that by 1977 a total of 5,878 people in the New Orleans metropolitan area would be working for the Defense Department, mostly the navy, and that the local economy would reap the benefits of a $100 million annual payroll.

"New Orleans will truly be a navy town," he triumphantly declared.

For achievements like these, plus his success at self-promotion, Hébert has been honored time and again by his constituents, but now he seems most appreciative of those tributes that would tend to immortalize him, those in which something is named after him.

There is Hébert Drive and Hébert Hall, the main roadway and the BOQ, respectively, at Alvin Callender Field, a largely unused air base that years ago Hébert had converted into a reserve training center for all of the service units in the area. Just inside the vestibule of Hébert Hall is a portrait of the congressman and a plaque. Below is a stool covered with velvet. Hébert jokingly says it's for genuflecting and calls it "the shrine."

Over in St. Bernard Parish, "Congressman Hébert

Drive" crosses in front of Chalmette National Cemetery, a burial ground which Hébert helped locate on the site of the Battle of New Orleans.

In neighboring Plaquemines Parish, the late Leander Perez, a one-time symbol of despotic segregationist rule, paid homage to his old friend and political ally by naming a major thoroughfare "F. Edward Hébert Boulevard."

In 1974 Hébert didn't let personal embarrassment or humility stand in the way of congressional friends pushing a bill to name the building in which his district office is located the "F. Edward Hébert Federal Building."

Tulane University showed its appreciation for the five hundred acres of surplus federal land he acquired for its new Science and Environmental campus by naming the facility the "F. Edward Hébert Center."

And for favors accorded that institution, Louisiana State University in New Orleans established the "F. Edward Hébert Library," which someday will be the recipient of the hundreds of mementos he has received. (Tulane has been promised his papers.)

Of course, his crowning pork barrel achievement, locating the reserve headquarters in New Orleans, was to be similarly recognized. Plans were afoot to call the site of the reserve headquarters the "F. Edward Hébert Defense Complex."

He has also sought immortality in the written word. In 1970, the University of Southwestern Louisiana published *Creed of a Congressman,* a collection of excerpts from Hébert letters and speeches, gathered together by an adoring professor, and prefaced by a forty-one-page biographical sketch written by his New Orleans executive assistant, Virginea Burguieres, an ex-newspaper woman. Not surprisingly, it reads like a hymnal.

In 1972 he began shopping around for a writer to do another book, one that would provide a fuller account of his life, including his chairmanship of the Armed Services Committee.

Needless to say, not everyone in New Orleans shares Hébert's view of himself. But he's unlikely to meet the dissenters. His circle of friends and political associates are homogeneous—white, middle-class to rich, middle-aged to elderly. The only blacks I saw at the host of functions in his honor were servicemen, who had to be there, one officer's wife and two ex-marines who were members of the corps' reserve unit.

Before their lunch at Brennan's, Hébert's party had cocktails in the lovely old courtyard of the restaurant. Not far away and at about the same time, blacks at the city council were angrily protesting a controversial police weapons firing policy. The one link between the two events was the council's most conservative member, a friend of Hébert's who arrived at Brennan's with a jovial account of the whole affair. That night in my hotel room I saw the scene on television. The hatred in the words and faces of the blacks was frightening and reminded me of the tensions in Washington four years earlier.

In 1972, blacks made up about half of New Orleans's population (although none sat on the council) and about 20 percent of Hébert's district. Just before a 1972 redistricting, it had been up to 25 percent. In terms of how he voted, Hébert had made no concessions to the Negro population.

"Sure, they're not crazy about my voting record. But I get along with the blacks. They know I bring them jobs. The only blacks I have trouble with in my district are the intellectuals. And they influence people down the line—the black press, the activists, the young people."

But he maintains a lot of working class blacks defend him, "in saloons and places like that. There are blacks who are very, very loyal to me. People I don't know by name. When they ask me about civil rights votes I tell them what I tell whites: you can't legislate civil rights."

He contends he's been getting a bum rap from black critics.

"I've opened the gates to blacks down there. Nobody's ever recognized it; nobody's ever said anything. I was the first to nominate them to the military academy. For years I've been nominating them. The first black Louisianan graduated from West Point two years ago. Got a black man there now."

He mentions another achievement: three of the twelve members of his staff are black. "But the militant will come back and say 'what's your administrative assistant?' No matter what you do, some of 'em you can't please. . . . I try to tell them I'm not a racist. But I'm not going to let the black organizations come into my office and tell me how to run it."

What Hébert neglects to add is that two of the three black staff members are his chauffeurs. The other is his liaison man with the black community, a venture which he concedes has not been entirely successful. But he blames this on the snobbishness of his black detractors. "They don't want him because he doesn't have a university degree."

Hébert has done much for New Orleans economically, but politically he is far removed from many of his constituents, white and black. He is not particularly close to local power blocs, such as New Orleans's progressive mayor, Moon Landrieu.

Hébert doesn't even get involved with those forces in the city which are on his side of the ideological spectrum. "He's entirely outside the city power structure, even as a conservative," said one local newsman. Why, then, I asked, hadn't the blacks, the moderates, the power structure, alone or collectively, ever tried to oust him? His answer boiled down to the undeniable fact that Hébert was unbeatable.

"He's an institution. Sort of an anachronistic one, but still an institution. He's too dug in and nobody wants to bother to try to unseat him. They'd rather wait until he goes and then replace him with someone who's more moderate and younger. And that's what his replacement will be."

By 1974 Eddie Hébert had done just about everything he would admit to ever having wanted to do. Two successful careers had brought him prominence, admiring friends and plenty of action. He has a fine wife and a daughter to whom he is close and who provided him with grandchildren. For most of his adult life there had been more than enough money to satisfy a healthy appetite for food, drink and a full range of comforts. And despite some threatening physical ailments, he by and large has managed to pull through with a level of pain and impairment that if not minimal is at least bearable.

Hébert succeeded because he was smart enough to spot and ride the tides, even when it appeared he was bucking them. The fighting editor who took on the Long machine knew he had the evidence and the support of the public when he went into battle. The young congressman who defied his party and president realized that his constituents were with him, and not Harry Truman. As long as he satisfied them and steered clear of traps laid by northern Democrats he would grow and prosper in his sanctuary on Capitol Hill.

In January, 1974, having inscribed his record on the rolls of powerful congressional committee chairmen, filled his district with all of the federal spoil it could handle and having done everything imaginable to confer immortality upon his name and accomplishments, F. Edward Hébert turned to the last item on his list.

Returning from a trip to New Orleans, he brought with him the news that he had just spent $15,500, "all cash," to buy a sarcophagus in a local mausoleum for him and Gladys. He disclosed the event with all of the delicacy one would employ in announcing the purchase of a condominium, thus assuring that the subject would be treated lightly. Lots of cracks followed but one gave him more of a kick than the others. He delighted in retelling it.

"You know what a friend of mine said? He said, 'what'd you spend all that money for? You're only going to be there three days.' Ain't that something?"

BENJAMIN S. ROSENTHAL

The dark-haired, intense, high school student stood up, pointed his finger at Benjamin Rosenthal and demanded to know how dare he attack President Nixon over Watergate!

In a fury of words, the young man spoke of 1938 and a ship filled with 2,500 Jews seeking entry into America and refuge from Hitler.

"But FDR and his Democratic liberal advisors said 'sorry, no Jews,'" he screamed.

"And 2,500 Jewish men, women and children were sent back to Germany. That's only the tip of the iceberg on how Roosevelt covered up the slaughter of the Jews.

"What about all the things the Democrats do? We hear nothing of this."

The student, with his short curly hair and white tennis sweater, looked incongruously like a chorus figure in a 1940 college movie. He wasn't finished.

"So don't come with the Democrats being so pious because you're not so perfect either."

The Honorable Benjamin Rosenthal, Democrat from New York's Eighth Congressional District, was back home in Queens, among his people.

It didn't always go like this. Often nice people did nice things, like the time the senior citizens group surprised him with a birthday cake. But nowadays there was no telling what he was likely to run into when he flew up from Washington.

In the Capitol, Rosenthal knew what to expect. There were his close friends, a small knot of issue-oriented Democratic liberals; many members who enjoyed his sense of humor and with whom he was on pleasant if not intimate terms; and his enemies. Over a period of ten years Benjamin Rosenthal had managed to amass a good-sized contingent of enemies. They have included:

Lyndon Johnson—who didn't like his early and constant criticism of U.S. policy in Vietnam.

John W. McCormack—who he unceremoniously and unsuccessfully tried to dump as Speaker in 1969.

Chet Holifield—with whom he fought bitterly over a consumer bill in 1971 and tried unsuccessfully to oust as chairman of the House Government Operations Committee in 1973.

Wayne Hays—an Ohio Democrat who makes lots of members mad and at whom Rosenthal almost threw a water pitcher.

James Delaney—a Democrat from a neighboring Queens district who got so worked up over Rosenthal's Vietnam stand that he reportedly took a swing at him. The two didn't speak to each other until the war was over.

John Wayne—who talked cowboy-tough to reporters

about what he would do to Rosenthal after the congressman criticized the government for the help it was giving Wayne in the filming of "The Green Berets."

Willie Mae Rogers—who lasted less than a week as President Nixon's first consumer advisor after Rosenthal criticized her because of her intention to remain as keeper of the Good Housekeeping Seal, whose award he linked to the amount of advertising a manufacturer placed in *Good Housekeeping* magazine.

If we accept the old adage that you can tell about a man from his enemies, we can learn even more from the institutions that Benjamin Rosenthal has enraged. They include:

The Chamber of Commerce and the National Association of Manufacturers—for his authorship and ardent advocacy of a sweeping consumer protection bill that they and other business groups contend would lock business into a mass of bureaucratic controls.

Supermarket chains—for his questioning of the safety and value of many of the foods they sell and for accusing some of stocking their ghetto outlets with food that was of lower quality and higher prices than that sold in higher income neighborhoods.

The Better Business Bureau—for his publication of a voluminous study a few years ago showing that in numerous cities the BBB served the business community rather than the consumer.

Mom and Pop drug store owners—for his proposal that prescription drug prices be advertised and that customers be given the right to buy drugs by generic names.

Cattle raisers—for his lead in organizing a housewives' meat boycott in 1973.

Users of Mexican stoop labor—for the role he played in 1963 in forcing an end to the "bracero" program under which American farmers imported Mexicans—rather than hire American migrant workers—to harvest their crops at substandard wages.

The general aviation industry—for his persistent efforts to close down Flushing Airport on grounds that the small private planes flying out of it are a threat to the safety of airliners using nearby LaGuardia Airport.

Rosenthal also has his friends and admirers. They include Ralph Nader, Bess Myerson, most consumer groups, pro-Israeli organizations, opponents of Greek military regimes, critics of Turkey's invasion of Cyprus, parliamentarian leaders of the European Common Market, old people, leftist thinkers, civil rights organizations, Kenneth Galbraith, Teddy Kennedy and John Lindsay.

And, finally, Rosenthal can claim detractors who are not enemies, people who don't object to his ideology or causes but who say he is too unyielding in pursuit of his goals. These include liberals who privately tell you that "Ben isn't willing to settle for half a loaf" or "Ben is too closely identified as an ultraliberal" or groups like the AFL-CIO-financed Consumers Federation of America, which leaned to Holifield rather than Rosenthal during their great battle of 1971.

And there are those who truly wish him well but who will say that he too often tries to blast his colleagues out of the cement in which they have planted themselves, when he should be chipping away a little at a time.

The object of all this enmity, affection and distress is an alternately wisecracking and moody 51-year-old man who is tall, skinny and round-shouldered. He has a small oval face, dominated by thick lips and dark horn-rimmed glasses. Come what may in the world of fashion, Ben Rosenthal wears his thinning and graying black hair straight back and short. His clothes are a little spiffier than Richard

Nixon's but not much. On a New York City scale they are not conservative Wall Street; neither are they up-town modish. They are Hart Schaffner and Marx's reliables.

Ben Rosenthal stormed into Congress on the crest of a 247-vote landslide, taking his seat on February 20, 1962, in the middle of the Eighty-seventh Congress. His predecessor had left to accept a state judgeship and Rosenthal had to beat out an independent Democrat as well as a Republican in the special election. He had been active in local politics but he had never held any elective office. That worked in his favor. After a stormy nominating session, the Democratic county executive committee decided on Rosenthal because he had fewer opportunities to make enemies than his five opponents.

He was not overwhelmed at his selection or at the prospect of going to the House. It wasn't that he lacked ambition. It was simply that things were going nicely in New York. He had come out of the army in 1946 (following eighteen months of duty as an MP in Iceland), gotten through City College of New York (CCNY) and Brooklyn Law School, married a slim, quiet and lovely girl named Leila Moskowitz and proceeded to build up a comfortable law practice in Elmhurst, Queens. Soon he would be moving his family to the suburbs farther out on Long Island.

Instead he found himself going south to Washington. And he went alone, because in 1962 New York City congressmen left their families at home, returning to them on extended weekends—three or four days—during which the representatives also tended to local political needs, their law practices and their constituents, usually in that order. Until John Lindsay brought his wife and children down in 1962, the New York delegation could claim 100 percent membership in the Tuesday-to-Thursday club. Rosenthal was the first Democrat to break the tradition. He did it in

1964, the same year that he hired a bright young man named Paul Gorman.

Before Gorman, Rosenthal ran his office like most of the New York machine Democrats ran theirs, staffing them with employees experienced in casework, local politics or both. Gorman, who was to later write speeches for presidential candidate Eugene McCarthy, was taken with concepts, issues and action. He introduced Rosenthal to the world of ideas and to the liberal thinkers who populated it, people like Marcus Raskin and Richard Barnett of the Institute for Policy Studies. The transition wasn't entirely smooth. For one thing, Gorman's enthusiastic brilliance unsettled the staff and at times even got to Rosenthal. "He told me he fired Paul a couple of times but he wouldn't go away," recalls Cliff Hackett, Gorman's successor.

But Rosenthal stuck to his new path. It led him to other Democratic liberals, men with ties to Americans for Democratic Action, university professors and the activists who were deep into the civil rights movement and asking their first hard questions about Vietnam. He learned that liberals outside of New York operated differently, and just as effectively.

"It helped broaden my view," he would say several years later. "I learned there was a country beyond the Hudson River. I saw that I could achieve something without making speeches."

On a summer morning in 1973, Ben Rosenthal picked me up on the way to work from his suburban home in Bethesda, Maryland. I wanted to see what congressmen do *all* day, not just at those times when reporters see them—at hearings, on the floor, at press conferences.

The ride was pleasant, through leafy, comfortable old neighborhoods of northwest Washington, down Rock Creek Parkway, along the handsome broad roads that pass by monuments. The car's air conditioning filtered out the heat and stickiness. Rosenthal agreed with me that congressional life in Washington could push aside unpleasant realities. He called the existence "a dream world" and recalled a tour he took a couple of years earlier in drug-devastated south Bronx.

"It's a jungle. You literally cannot safely walk the streets in the middle of the day." He repeated the same sentence, slower and louder. (When Rosenthal wants to make a point —which can be often—he abandons contractions, and carefully enunciates his words, New York accent and all, like a teacher desperately striving to make his students understand.)

As we drove, he talked about a hearing he would be holding that morning before his European affairs subcommittee, the chairmanship of which he inherited in 1971 when House Democratic reforms redistributed power in committees. For months he had been using the subcommittee post to hammer away at the administration's policy toward the Greek junta, and particularly at a United States decision to build a permanent naval facility there for ships of the American Sixth Fleet.

Shortly after 9 A.M. we pulled into the Rayburn Building garage, parked, took an elevator to the fourth floor and walked into his three-room suite. He grunted to his receptionist, a young, curvy redhead (like many other members, he's always managed to find pretty young women for the front office), and picked up his one telephone message. Inside his office the mail was stacked on a table in boxes, labeled "Case," "Legislative" and "General." Rosenthal says he reads all his mail. He goes out to "steal" a cigarette, the first of three or four that he will bum during the day, looks through the paper work piled on his desk, wanders in and out of the office, dropping off material with staff members as he does so. Everyone is working quietly. Rosenthal is less jolly and more pensive in the office than he is elsewhere in the Capitol. No kidding around like Hébert. He gives directions somewhat curtly, especially to women, whom he concedes he's not very good at handling. The two men on his staff—Peter Barash and Doug Bloomfield—address him as "Ben." All of the women, including those older than the men and one who makes more money, address him as "Congressman" or "Mr. Rosenthal." This touch of sexism has its humorous aspect. I once bumped into Rosenthal in the Capitol while he was talking to Rep. Patricia Schroeder. Ever the issue-conscious liberal, he seriously spoke to her of the need for a "congressperson" at an upcoming function.

I told him I was struck by the efficiency of his staff, that it seemed as if it could almost perform without him. He agreed, noting how self-sustaining a congressional office could be if a member chose to concentrate exclusively on servicing constitutents and avoided the type of activity that Rosenthal seeks out. "I figure I could be sick and away from the Capitol for six months and 90 percent of the people back home wouldn't know I had been out unless they checked the roll calls."

The casework, administrative and secretarial chores in the office are supervised by Mary Davis, a cheerful, efficient woman who worked for Rosenthal's predecessor. She knows the district, the Hill and the bureaucracy. Six or seven women work under her. During the summer, the staff is augmented by a number of student interns who are willing to work hard and want to learn about politics. Of the two men on his Washington staff, Barash is a young lawyer and Bloomfield an even younger ex-reporter with the Cleveland *Plain Dealer* who came to Washington via an American Political Science Association (APSA) fellowship and decided to stay with Rosenthal after spending part of his year with him. Barash had worked for Rosenthal as a member of the Government Operations Committee staff, but he drew the ire of Chairman Holifield for his Nader-like approach to consumer issues, and his future on the committee was grim. Rosenthal put him on his personal staff, where, coincidentally, the congressman was forced to do all his consumer muckracking after Holifield dissolved the special consumer affairs panel Rosenthal headed.

That action set off a series of wars between Holifield and Rosenthal. Holifield won almost all of them, but not without cost. After waiting twenty-two years as second ranking Democrat to become chairman, Holifield discovered that life at the top of the House Government Operations Committee was not much fun because of gadflies like Rosenthal.

Holifield was an old line, cold war liberal—solid on civil rights and welfare programs, just as solid on a strong military establishment and an aggressive foreign policy. With the passing of time, Holifield found himself more often resisting change than demanding it.

In 1973 Rosenthal asked the Democratic caucus—the organization of all the House Democrats—to take the almost unprecedented step of ousting Holifield from his Government Operations Committee chairmanship. In a well-documented brief sent to all of his colleagues, Rosenthal argued that Holifield had held back the committee from exercising its responsibilities as the House's principal watchdog over government activities. As expected, the caucus generally ignored the brief, stuck with tradition and overwhelmingly rejected Rosenthal's move.

Rosenthal finally got rid of his antagonist in 1974 when a

California redistricting plan discouraged the 73-year-old Holifield from seeking reelection. Ironically, in his last year Holifield worked out a compromise with Rosenthal over the consumer protection agency bill, the measure which had generated their deepest and bitterest conflicts. The House passed the legislation with the two antagonists complimenting each other's statesmanship. Unfortunately for both, as well as the country, the measure died in a Senate filibuster.

Shortly before ten o'clock we took the elevator down to the Foreign Affairs Committee hearing room. There we were met by Cliff Hackett, Rosenthal's subcommittee staff specialist. A former Foreign Service officer, Hackett came to the Hill in 1966 on an APSA fellowship, worked with Rosenthal part of the year and, as Bloomfield would later, decided to stay. Slender, goateed, in his early forties, he furnishes Rosenthal with competent and imaginative staff assistance, encourages him to launch ground-breaking ventures and helps him keep a sense of humor and perspective by reminding the congressman of the comic side of the predicaments the two occasionally get themselves into.

The hearing turned out to be a wasted hour. The State Department witness, a last minute substitute for the official who was scheduled to appear, did not have the experience or standing to take on aggressive congressmen, particularly those who knew their subject. Making matters worse, the State Department privately was unhappy with the navy's insistence on establishing a home port in Greece but was forced to remain silent and publicly endorse the proposal. The subcommittee pressed the witness but got little more than lame responses. When it became apparent that there was no point in going further, Rosenthal banged his gavel and summarily adjourned the hearing.

The rest of the day, by Rosenthal's standards, was unusually light. We ate lunch at a small table in the House dining room. Bill Alexander, the young Democrat from Arkansas who was showing signs of growing activism, dropped by and Rosenthal asked him to join us. Alexander is polite but today he was mad. Holifield, it seems, was causing problems for Arkansas moderates as well as New York ultraliberals. Alexander was having trouble getting Holifield's authorization to attend the Geneva Disarmament Conference, in the same way Patricia Schroeder was having trouble with Hébert, and he suspected Holifield was trying to punish him for a vote or two he had recently cast in committee.

"He and others don't seem to realize there's a new breed around, people who don't think they should have to make deals to do your job," said Alexander. "If you want to do something for your country or your district and you're not a chairman you run into a brick wall. The only way you don't is if you're a 'go-along, get-along' type. You know what they are. They're wagon dogs, as we say in Arkansas." Later I asked Rosenthal how well he knew Alexander. "I know I like him," he answered.

After lunch Rosenthal met with the six interns who were working on his staff for the summer. Each had been assigned a project, usually a consumer related investigation, given a crash course in research techniques by Barash and Bloomfield, and turned loose. Today they were providing Rosenthal with progress reports. He told me that often students' findings served as a basis for his legislative programs.

Except for a couple of floor votes on relatively minor legislation, the afternoon was free—for an ice cream sundae (a daily obsession with Rosenthal) and paddle ball in the House gym. Like many other lawmakers, he finds the game

—a form of handball played with paddles—physically stimulating and mentally relaxing. He likes it for another reason too, one that would appeal to marginal athletes.

"I now have an inalienable right to play in a game. As a kid I was always left out or on the bench. I came down here and they've got a system where the guy who runs the gym matches you up with whomever is waiting. Sometimes I'm over my head but I've gotten better, and developed confidence.

"It's also a nice opportunity to socialize and set up a potential legislative dialogue with people you normally don't deal with."

Most often, however, he plays with his three close friends and ideological allies, Robert Kastenmeier of Madison, Wisconsin, Don Edwards, a congressman from southern California and Donald Fraser, representative from Minneapolis. They drew Rosenthal into tennis, which he plays with grim determination if not polish.

Around 5:30 P.M. he left the office to meet his wife at the Irish Embassy for a reception given by the ambassador. He gained the admiration of the embassy a few years ago when he held hearings on the Ulster turmoil, hearings that were overtly sympathetic to the Irish Republic and the Catholics of Northern Ireland.

Despite his perennial battling with men and institutions and the periods of physical and emotional weariness it produces, Rosenthal does a lot of kidding around. If he's not arguing, exploding or moaning he's wisecracking. At times it seems as if he can't take his own proposals seriously. At a news conference he'll open up by trading quips with reporters. He often does the same with cabinet witnesses who sit before him at hearings. It's hard to say whether his lines are funny. He delivers them with utter confidence, not dreaming that they would fall flat, and moves on. The humor is vintage New York-Jewish, moderately sophisticated. He applies it to everyone, even Holifield.

"You know what he did today," he told a reporter interviewing him the day before the caucus was to meet on his dump-Holified move, "he came up to me on the floor and said, 'hello Benjamin.' That's the first time he's called me by my Christian name—so to speak."

Rosenthal's usual state of good cheer helps take the edges off the contentiousness of some of his legislative crusades and what he regards as his tendency to annoy people now and then. He also tries to counter it by avoiding a stereotype.

"You can't be up there every day on everything, in every battle. You've got to pick and choose. It's a concern—if you're too heavy, too frequent, too often, too New York, too Jewish, it doesn't help.

"But still, the more you do, the more people you bruise. It's inevitable. You try to do what you do in a reasonable style. I do think there are some people who think I'm abrasive. In some ways I think I am abrasive. It's true. You know you can't change your personality."

He admires and envies the style of Don Fraser, a liberal who can say, "the wildest things," but because he presents them in a calm, reasoned manner no one gets upset. "And he's not looked upon as a self-immolating radical. It's his style."

Nevertheless, Rosenthal believes he's making progress. He'll now stay out of a debate when he feels it's going along well without him. During a particularly critical fight over Vietnam policy in 1973, Rosenthal sat silent while the fund-cutoff case was argued by Georgia's John Flynt.

"When you've got a guy like John Flynt on your side you shut up."

Bella Abzug and Ronald Dellums took the floor during the same debate. It's highly doubtful whether they converted anyone to their side. It's possible they drove some away. Probably neither was the case, but they decided they had as much right to speak as anyone else and they did. Rosenthal accepts this motivation and also recognizes that perhaps their constituents expect it of them. But he faults it on tactical grounds. He is proud that he has learned to work with conservatives on his committees, men like John Buchanan, a Republican from Alabama who serves on his European affairs subcommittee, and John Erlenborn, an Illinois Republican from Government Operations. He finds both of them intelligent and open-minded. On occasion they can get together on an issue and more frequently on an important committee procedure.

But appreciating all this, Rosenthal still can blow it, through stubbornness, pride or, as a friend put it, an inability or unwillingness to ingratiate himself with people he doesn't know, and sometimes doesn't like, in a bid for their support.

In the fall of 1973 he learned, apparently through some poignant personal contacts with constituents, of the harsh toll inflation was taking on the elderly. He came back to Washington and hit upon the idea of speeding up by half a year a planned boost in Social Security benefits. He contacted Hubert Humphrey and the two mapped out a joint strategy. Humphrey took care of the Senate; Rosenthal went after the House. He lined up more than one hundred cosponsors to his proposal and then devised a tricky parliamentary scheme to get the measure through. He went to the Democratic leadership and persuaded it to push ahead, both for humanitarian and political reasons. He didn't, however, clear his plans with Wilbur Mills, the potent chairman of the Ways and Means Committee, which has jurisdiction over Social Security. Caught up in the flush of activity and his early successes, he couldn't be bothered with ironing out the prospective parliamentary problems with Mills.

"That's the leadership's worry," he told me, adding that he couldn't imagine Mills causing any difficulty simply over pride or jurisdiction.

"Maybe not, but how do you know he won't turn it down on grounds there's no money to pay for it?"

"That's too goddamn bad," he answered irritably. "I've got old people in my district who don't have the money to buy enough food. Let them find the money."

In the end, a variation of the Social Security speedup was enacted, but it wasn't as liberal as Rosenthal's, his having been pushed aside weeks before—after Mills insisted upon working it out his way.

Ben and Leila Rosenthal do not live opulently. But they do live nicely. They enjoy the familiar comforts of an upper middle class existence in the suburbs—two cars, membership in an expensive country club and two vacations a year. (The availability of congressional junkets enables them to travel abroad at considerably less expense than most Americans do, although Rosenthal says the trips usually leave him with little time for recreation.)

The Rosenthals readily concede that they live well. But in 1973 they said they were approaching the point where they would be living beyond their means. Acknowledging that it sounded slightly absurd, they told me that unless congressional salaries were boosted—they hadn't been since rising to $42,500 in 1969—their upcoming annual vacation at Palm Beach would be their last for awhile. Like many people, they had been spending most of what was coming in and it no longer was enough to sustain the standard of living they had adopted. One of their two children was in college and the other would be in a few years. And because Rosenthal is forever pushing issues that require large-scale mailings, he must dip into his own pocket to subsidize printing costs when his government stationery allowance runs out, which he says is often.

Rosenthal's 1973 statement of financial holdings, filed with the House Ethics Committee, listed an interest in two mutual funds and one investment club. (House rules do not require disclosure of the size of the interest or the amounts of any income derived from it.) On June 3, 1974, *The New York Times* published what financial information members of the New York delegation were willing to make public about themselves. Rosenthal declined to list his net worth but he did disclose that his adjusted gross income in 1973 was $44,070 ($1,570 more than his congressional salary) and on which he paid $9,782 in taxes.

He gave up a partnership in his old law firm a few years ago after reading a Bar Association report contending that members of Congress who continue their association with a law firm lay themselves open to a conflict of interest. Rosenthal looked back on his own experience and concluded that the report was right.

"Even unintentionally your influence can get involved. My partner can be working on some stupid real estate deal and needs a Veteran's Administration loan expedited. Without him saying anything, the guy at the VA knows he's with a congressman and he'll get special treatment."

Rosenthal represents a district that is heavily Jewish,

decidedly liberal and overwhelmingly Democratic. Thus it's hardly a surprise that a Democratic Jewish liberal would do well there. Rosenthal has done extremely well. In 1972, he won reelection with nearly 65 percent of the vote. Richard Nixon carried the district by 51 percent—which indicates how George McGovern was received in a district that had been carved to order for Democratic candidates. Nevertheless, Rosenthal linked his campaign closely to McGovern's, turning out campaign brochures that prominently featured pictures of the two of them shaking hands.

Rosenthal has not had a tough race since his first one, in 1962. Yet he still runs as if there was some doubt about the outcome.

"In 1972 I spoke every day like crazy. I had headquarters and people and station wagons and signs. Sure I knew, or at least surmised, that I wouldn't need all that. But you can't lay down, because if you do you'll invite primary opposition. You just got to show the world you can do it. And you got to keep your people. People want to work. But you have to have work for them to do. They don't want to sit around. You can't tell them there's nothing to do."

Rosenthal disregards the conventional wisdom of the Hill that in order to stay in office a congressman has to pay close personal attention to casework. He has found that with rare exceptions his staff can handle individual problems as well as he can. This frees him to concentrate on national issues that have an impact on his district, such as consumer affairs. He inspired a well-publicized, nationwide meat boycott in 1973 in response to the complaints he received from shoppers in his district. The ensuing publicity boosted his image still higher at home.

I asked him why he worked so hard when he had such a safe seat.

"I have a safe seat *because* I work hard," he answered.

In 1970 he won reelection with 63 percent of the vote. Two years later, after a redistricting that he figured left him with about the same ratio of friendly to unfriendly voters he had before, he bucked the anti-McGovern swing and upped his victory margin to 64.8 percent. In 1974 it was 78 percent. He's had no competition from fellow Democrats for the nomination since his early days and he's had no serious threat in the general election, though a large enough pocket of conservative, working-class sentiment exists in the district to prompt the Republican and Conservative parties to run candidates against him.

A map of the Eighth Congressional District of New York looks like a giant lobster claw plunked down on northwestern Long Island, pincering a chunk of Flushing as it reaches eastward to the edge of Nassau County. The area includes such nationally known features as Shea Stadium; Flushing Meadows, site of the 1939 and 1964 World's Fairs; the approach pattern to LaGuardia Airport and the neighborhood which provided the film footage for the introductory scene to the "All in the Family" television program. A lot of Archie Bunkers live in Rosenthal's district—he was censured by local veterans' groups for his antiwar activities—but they are in a minority, and Rosenthal felt that in 1974 with the war over and the racial tensions that had been plaguing New York easing a bit, he was beginning to reach them.

Most of the people in his district live in middle-class apartments packed into sections like Flushing, Forest Hills, Fresh Meadows and Bayside. Blue-collar constituents and their families live to the west, in places like Elmhurst and Woodside, near the light industry of Long Island City, and Sunnyside that sits astride the East River across from Manhattan. In between are black neighborhoods, located mostly in Corona and Elmhurst. The black population makes up about 5 percent of the total.

🚩

In order to see Rosenthal in action at home, I flew to New York early one Friday morning in May, 1973, to spend a day with him there. Coincidentally, his district included that part of Flushing where I was born and raised, not far from the Post Office on Main Street where his office is located.

Rosenthal's district operations consisted mostly of casework and dealings with community groups, handled by a staff of five, all but two of whom worked part time. His district representative was Mike Goldenthal, who the Friday I was there was preparing for his wedding on Sunday. Inside Rosenthal's office, an unembellished, two-room suite, were three women—his principal office aide, Francine Siedlecki, a vibrant woman in her late twenties who left teaching for politics after a stint toiling for George McGovern's 1968 presidential candidacy; Ann Schachter, an official in the local party organization, who worked three days a week, and Rachel Gordon, a young and pretty law school student who had served as one of his interns in Washington the summer before.

Because they were used to being on their own for most of the week and probably because they were in New York, the atmosphere was a bit looser than it was in Washington.

"Where's the memo for the meeting with the principals?" he asks.

"They never sent it from Washington."

"Oh, Geez."

"Why don't you just wing it?"

"I'm not kidding now."

"I can imagine."

"It's partially your fault, why didn't you . . ."

"I sent down a note last week, with a copy to you, asking for it," she wailed. "How much more can I do?"

Wearily and softly Rosenthal replies: "You can follow up."

They carry on a bit more, deescalating the conflict with reminders that the Washington staffer that was supposed to have handled the task was out sick two days and that Rosenthal was too distracted by other matters to check on it. A call is made to Washington to get the information. The family is put together again.

But other calamities bob to the surface as the day wears on, ranging from why-isn't-there-any-coffee-for-the-principals to Rosenthal's perpetual, all-consuming determination to reduce the telephone bill.

"I'm serious. I'm not fooling around. We're over our allowance. There can be no personal calls. None. Is that clear? None. And you call Washington only when it is necessary. I'm serious."

Rosenthal's first appointment of the day was with the representative of a railway workers union local who sought his support for bills improving employees' pensions and providing subsidies for the northeastern railroads. Rosenthal didn't commit himself, saying he first wanted to study the measures more closely, but indicated he was sympathetic and probably would vote for them. They got along well.

After he left I told Rosenthal I was struck by how familiar the man, a rail-yard worker, was with the subject matter.

"It's an interesting thing. You meet a lot of people in New York City—you don't as much in Washington—who are deeply committed to their unions. Their whole lives are tied up with belonging to the union. They read everything that comes out. This guy is not a professional. He's a regular worker. Actually, that is the strength of the union movement, that they have a lot of nonpaid people very much into it. Where the union movement gets weak is where you have all these goddamn paid union staff organizers, who are no longer workers. They build a union bureaucracy which is just as decadent and as inflexible as management bureaucracy."

His cynicism about big labor in Washington was not surprising. Besides the AFL-CIO's tolerance of Vietnam, and its opposition to the McGovern candidacy, the federation had drawn Rosenthal's annoyance in 1971 when it took an ambivalent position on the consumer bill he and Ralph Nader were trying desperately to get through the House.

Next came a shy, English-born lady from the American Association of University Women. Her organization was sounding out lawmakers on a variety of environmental issues and her assignment was to interview Rosenthal. The session ended with his giving her tips on who her group should work on in Washington.

The conference with the principals from the seven public high schools in the district was part of a program Rosenthal had recently launched to develop closer ties with different segments of the community and to find out what he could do in Washington to help with their problems. A couple of weeks earlier he had held a similar exchange of views with police officials and implied to me that as one who viewed crime from the perspective of a civil libertarian and social reformer he found the experience enlightening.

"I was surprised at the quality and caliber of the guys. They were nice guys. They were guys who say, 'Look, I'm hired to do a job. When somebody commits a crime, I do my job. Don't tell me about society. If *you* want to do something about society, okay. But that's not my job.' They seemed intelligent, bright. Some had been up all night. I was surprised. They weren't fat old buffoons. They were very professional."

The principals were less surprising to him, probably not surprising at all. They were people Rosenthal knew and understood. All but one—the single woman among them—were Jewish, reflecting the movement of Jews into the New York City school system. But now, rather than preparing Jewish and other youngsters for college or vocational careers, they were also coping with the problems of integrating students of different races and economic levels in a city whose melting pot traditions had harshly given way to tension and defensiveness, to painful conflicts such as the teachers' strike of 1968.

Less than an hour later Rosenthal ran into a nonviolent confrontation—from an unexpected direction. It took place at Cardozo High School in Bayside, where he had been invited to address the school's social studies classes. The seven-year-old, low-slung building housed 3,600 students, taught in two sessions. Jewish kids were the largest single group. Black students generally kept to themselves, but no tension was evident the day we stopped by.

The session was held in an amphitheater-style lecture room, filled with about 200 students and teachers. Rosenthal promptly took off his jacket, put one foot up on a chair, delivered a few opening remarks and asked for questions.

The televised hearings of the Ervin Committee had just begun so Watergate came up quickly. Without any qualifications, Rosenthal branded it and the related scandals a monstrous event in American history and held President Nixon accountable for the atmosphere which permitted it to occur. Impeachment at the time was still a remotely considered outcome, and Rosenthal's ready acknowledgment of its possibility triggered some resentment among those who had backed Nixon in the previous election. At one point, a middle-aged male teacher told Rosenthal he didn't see much difference between the Watergate offenses and the political crimes that netted Bobby Baker thousands of dollars during the days of Lyndon Johnson. Rosenthal exploded.

"Let me tell what I think of that line. I think it's a lot of crap."

Some "oohed"; others clapped. He went on.

"That's the Ronald Reagan line: 'These weren't really criminals. They weren't stealing money. They were doing it for a higher cause. They're not guilty of anything.'

"Sure there are lots of politicians who steal money and feather their own nests. But I find this far more offensive—the arrogance and usurpation of power. This divine right to do anything they want, that they're above the law. And then sell that power to the highest bidder—to Vesco for $50,000 and to the milk producers for $200,000 and to Dwayne Andreas for $25,000 for a bank charter."

A few moments later, as he was about to answer another question, Rosenthal's political instincts returned and he apologized to the teacher.

"I didn't mean to be offensive," he said.

"You were offensive," said the still unmollified teacher. "In fact, you used the same tactics you were accusing Nixon of."

Rosenthal continued to receive questions about Watergate and hammered away at what he contended was the enormity of the scandal. But he also spoke of the cleansing effect he predicted it would have on American politics, government and society. He made some predictions which at the time seemed like hyperbole but, in retrospect, were eerily prescient.

"The word 'Watergate' will join our vocabulary like the word 'gerrymander.' It will come to symbolize corruption in government . . . corruption of power. . . . We're going to go through the most convulsive, disturbing, painful period in the history of the country. We're going to see a recounting of the most dastardly political acts this country has ever seen."

Someone asked whether Spiro Agnew would be connected to Watergate—this was well before the vice-president's own troubles had surfaced. Rosenthal said he personally did not think so but that if it was shown to be the case he thought Agnew would be forced to resign. "You're going to see some unusual, wildly unspiraling events." He closed on a positive note, claiming that the whole experience would serve as a catharsis, with resulting reforms in politics and government and a restoration of the rights of individual privacy.

Most of the audience accepted his thesis. One did not.

A boy of about seventeen stood up. Speaking with the slightest trace of a European accent, his eyes flashing, he began stiffly and formally.

"I wish to point up another case of political corruption. . ." He went on to describe the shipload of German Jews who sought refuge in America in 1938.

"What about all the things the Democrats do?" he asked. Rosenthal tried to answer but the boy kept on, becoming more excited. "We hear nothing of this." Other kids in the audience stirred and one shouted, "Give him a chance to answer." Teachers shushed for quiet.

Rosenthal, speaking softly, said he was familiar with the history that embraced such incidents, that he found Arthur Morse's book, *How Six Million Died* to be an excellent source. But he said he didn't see the relationship between that crime and Watergate. Then he added:

"You're quite right though. Sumner Welles and his people misled Roosevelt." The concession gave the kid another opening, another chance to reopen the battle.

"So don't come with the Democrats being so pious, because you're not so perfect either."

"You're quite right," Rosenthal said. "I didn't mean to be so pious. But I don't think anyone, be he Republican or liberal, should condone Watergate. Nor do I think anyone should condone the incident you spoke of."

After the session at the high school, as Rachel drove us back to the office, Rosenthal criticized himself for blowing up at the teacher. Rachel brought up the student questioner, who it was agreed could have been a member of the Jewish Defense League.

"It's a good thing you didn't talk about Soviet Jewry," she said.

"You're not kidding."

"Do you run across that kind very often?" I asked him.

"You run across one of everything at every meeting."

"How do you classify that kid?"

"That's a JDL ball breaker. That issue transcends all others. All I know is that he's an absolute hardliner. A guy like me, a liberal Democrat—he hates me."

"Even though you're a Jew?"

"He hates me more *because* I'm a Jew."

"The Jewish activists are taking no more crap from anyone on anything," he added. "In a sense they have a point."

For the rest of the afternoon, Rosenthal did two interviews on consumerism, one for WCBS-TV, another with a woman writing for a feature service. Things had quieted down and, as often happens with Rosenthal, unless something comes along to perk him up, the fatigue from pre-

vious efforts settles in and he takes on an uninterested, uninteresting quality. He suggested we pop across the street to
an ice cream parlor for a malt. It helped. He joked with two
mothers treating their children to sundaes and on the way
back stopped to meet the new postmaster in his building.
He declined Fran Siedlecki's suggestion that he place a con-
gratulatory call to the newly named Queens County district
attorney, a man he barely knew.

"No, I'm not gonna. That's ass-kissing stuff."

He was about to lapse into weariness again when he was
roused out of his lethargy by his next appointment—
Gerald Gold, recently appointed consumer affairs editor
of *The New York Times*. It was more than the presence of
The Times that energized him. Gold, a large, jolly man
who was making a get-acquainted call, quickly established
a loose rapport with Rosenthal and in moments it was apparent that the two had hit it off well and had established
a solid working relationship.

After Gold left, Rosenthal called it a day. It was about
5:30, and he planned to attend a stag party that evening for
his about-to-be-married chief district aide.

Over the years Rosenthal has come to the conclusion that
the seniority system is the endemic weakness of the House.
That is not a novel conclusion. But he sees a dimension to
it that is not usually mentioned by most critics.

Not only does seniority permit individuals of small accomplishment to attain positions of importance and power,
but it leads to a rule by people well past their prime.

"At forty-nine years old," he said of himself, "where else
can you be described as 'young!' Only here. It's an unreal
place."

In 1971, at the age of 62, Carl Albert became the Speaker of the House of Representatives. Rosenthal, who thought little of Albert's predecessor, John McCormack, looked forward to Albert. But soon it became apparent that Albert was not going to live up to the expectations of those seeking an innovative, dynamic leader. Although disappointed, Rosenthal said he wasn't surprised. He recognized Albert as a man of intelligence, depth and sensitivity. But for nine years, while he filled the position of majority leader, Albert obediently served a man of John McCormack's stature, not daring to speak or act on his own for fear it would be interpreted as disloyalty.

"When it was time for him to take over he had atrophied," Rosenthal said. "What corporation would wait until a man is sixty-two before moving him to the presidency?" he asked, citing the age Albert became Speaker. (He could have mentioned McCormack, who was seventy when he succeeded Sam Rayburn.)

Most of Rosenthal's congressional career in Washington has been spent taking on the old order. First it's asking, then cajoling, then pushing and finally saying, the hell with it, and whacking away at them. He could almost bear putting up with it all if it was limited to the big issues and to doing combat with the Republicans.

"But it's the hocking you have to do over the little things. To get a decent hearing room. The fighting you have to do with people in your own party. It wears you out."

"They're grinding him down, there's no doubt about it," says Peter Barash. "But it's amazing how resilient he is. He keeps bouncing back."

Yet Rosenthal worries that if he stays in the House he will eventually stop bouncing back, that slowly but surely he will succumb to the fear of change, which he sees as an almost inevitable accompaniment to age and longevity in a place like Congress. He remembers that Chet Holifield was once known as a liberal activist.

One day in the late 1960s I met Rosenthal for lunch. We walked from his office to a small Italian tavern that fixed sandwiches he liked. On the way he told me of an article he had just read, about men who had switched careers in mid-life and had found the transformation exhilarating. He was going through a head-knocking period in the House at the time and the idea sounded intriguing. He thought that maybe he was ready to quit Congress and try something else. Perhaps teaching.

In 1973 we ate together again. This time we were with our wives and we dined at an expensive French restaurant in downtown Washington. Without intentionally underscoring the irony of the two locales, I reminded him of our conversation at Jimmy's several years earlier. Did he still consider quitting?

He didn't answer directly. But he made it clear it was no longer a realistic possibility. He spoke frankly of his investment in the congressional pension plan and what it would mean to the financial security of his family. "It's not inconsequential. Each year you stay means a lot." And as much as he despised it, his returns were coming in on his involuntary investment in the seniority system. He was a subcommittee chairman now. Foreign governments, the State Department, journalists took him seriously. If he hung around long enough, I thought to myself, it would be conceivable he could become chairman of the Foreign Affairs Committee.

"You know," he said, "you become a captive to the place."

7

Evicting a Tenant

"IT IS NONE of their business."

Rumpled old Byron Rogers was distressed. Mendel Rivers was beside himself. Colmer of Mississippi was defiant. It was outrage time in the House, and once again the target was the courts. This time it wasn't what the courts had done, but what they might do.

The date was March 9, 1967. Eight days earlier, members had decided that Adam Clayton Powell no longer belonged in their midst and they had formally denied him the seat he had legitimately won in the November election. Never one to slip quietly away, lick his wounds, accept defeat and, in this instance, collect his handsome pension, Powell did the unprecedented: he asked the judiciary to inject itself into an "internal matter" of Congress. Specifically, he wanted a federal judge to say that the House acted unconstitutionally when it "excluded' him from the Ninetieth Congress. He wanted the judge to issue an order directing the House's leaders and officials to readmit him with full pay, rank and privileges.

167

It wasn't as if anyone took the move seriously. Even those who had voted on March 1 to seat Powell knew his suit wasn't going anywhere. And many of them didn't think it ought to. Separation of powers was a three-sided doctrine. If the Constitution forced the House and Senate to swallow the indignity of a single judge declaring their legislative work invalid, if it required them to sit by and do nothing while a president met their request for information with an imperial invocation of executive privilege, well then, they sure as hell had a right to run their own affairs without interference from the courts or anyone else.

As a matter of equity, the theory sounded fine. What most members ignored, or failed to grasp, was that the House was more than an institution locked in battle with two other institutions. It was also, as its name clearly indicated, *the* place in government which under the Constitution represented citizens.

Probably more than any other event in House history, the action taken against Powell and his constituents illustrated the quaint, debilitating and dangerous notion of many members that besides reflecting national views, the House served as the private club of its occupants. Thus on March 9, one member after another rose to denounce the heretic assertion that the House was limited in its power to discipline its own. The debate that day took on the air of an angry fraternity meeting, with members citing sections of the Constitution as if they were the group's bylaws.

The degree of the House's paranoia on the issue could be measured by listening to the debate. No one supported Powell's legal position. Everyone who spoke agreed that it was preposterous. The debate revolved around the question of whether to send lawyers to court and tell the judge that or to simply ignore the suit, refusing to even dignify it by responding. The leaders, both Democratic and Republican, thought the sensible thing to do was for attorneys to represent the House and forcefully argue that the courts had no jurisdiction in the matter. They were confident no sane judge would conclude otherwise.

But not everybody saw it that way. Merely showing up in court, warned Mendel Rivers, might give a judge the idea that the House saw merit in Powell's case. William Colmer, the crusty seventy-seven-year-old chairman of the Rules Committee, breathed fire. He urged the House to follow the example of Andrew Jackson, who responded to a Supreme Court ruling of 1832 with the historic declaration: "Well John Marshall has made his decision, now let him enforce it."*

Let a federal judge anywhere in the land hand down a decision that threatens the independence of the national legislature and invariably someone in the House takes the floor and invokes Jackson. Usually the orator hasn't the vaguest notion of what the Johnson-Marshall controversy was all about.

It was left to Byron Rogers, Democrat from Colorado, however, to put forth the most novel proposal. Rogers was a senior member of the Judiciary Committee and a former attorney general of Colorado. But he looked and sounded more like a kindly, old, slightly befuddled proprietor of a general store.

---

* In fact, the decision represented an attempt by the Supreme Court to reinforce the position of both the executive branch, which is charged with executing laws, and the legislative branch, which is responsible for writing them. In violation of U.S.-Indian treaties, and an 1802 Act of Congress, the state of Georgia had been exercising jurisdiction over Indian lands within the state. Georgia had defied writs of the Supreme Court, imprisoned and even executed some Cherokees that its courts had convicted of crimes. Although the essential legal authority of the federal government was at stake, Jackson wasn't about to send in troops and risk an armed clash with Georgia. His reelection campaign was coming up, neighboring South Carolina was seeking allies in its nullificaton drive and besides, Jackson didn't hanker much to Indians.

"What would be wrong," Rogers wanted to know, "with the Speaker writing a little letter down here to the judge and saying, 'I am a member of the House, the Speaker of the House of Representatives, and I am not subject to this suit. Will you therefore excuse me and the remainder of the members? Why can't we do that?"

Finally the leaders prevailed, convincing the members, in the words of Gerald Ford, that "as a practical matter, there has to be someone to go down there and tell them it is none of their business."

A few minutes later the House voted itself permission to draw on the Treasury for open-ended legal defense fund. Of course the Justice Department maintained a stable of constitutional attorneys who were already being paid by the taxpayers. But the elders felt that since the House's first line of defense was based on the separation of powers principle, it would be more appropriate to retain private counsel.

With that the House went out and hired the most expensive lawyers it could find.* They were to do battle with a ragtag band of Howard University law professors and prominent activist attorneys such as William Kunstler and Arthur Kinoy who had volunteered to represent Powell.

---

* The arrangement turned out to be an unhappy one for the House, the taxpayers and the two law firms involved, Cravath, Swaine and Moore of New York, and Wilmer, Cutler and Pickering of Washington. After two-thirds of the litigation had been completed, the attorneys submitted a bill for $213,055.30. It was quietly approved by the House Administration Committee and paid. Press disclosure of payment, however, prompted members like Wayne Hays, one of those who had approved it, to take to the floor and charge that the House had been gouged. No record can be found that the House ever received or paid a bill for the remainder of the services rendered. And the lawyers, even five years later, refused to discuss the matter, contending that it would violate their profession's canons. My own suspicion is that the firms decided to absorb the cost themselves rather than endure another round of unseemly and public name-calling by their clients.

Powell had lost his seat following two House investigations, which charged him with having taken some highly pleasurable and strictly personal trips at taxpayer expense to his retreat on the Bahamian isle of Bimini. The traveling had been falsely attributed to staff members, according to the investigators. Powell was also accused of having illegally kept his estranged wife on the congressional payroll and of having exhibited "contumacious" conduct toward the courts of New York State.

Powell was not ousted from the House. He was excluded. The difference is more than semantic. On January 10, 1967, he presented himself along with more than 430 other members-elect to be sworn into the Ninetieth Congress. Rep. Lionel Van Deerlin, a little known Democrat from San Diego, objected to Powell taking the oath, on grounds that he was a fugitive from justice, having been held in contempt of court for persistently refusing to pay a judgment awarded to a Harlem widow whom Powell had slandered. The House ordered Powell to step aside while a specially created committee looked into his behavior.

In addition to examining the history of his battle with the New York courts, the panel, headed by Judiciary Committee Chairman Emanuel Celler, reviewed the evidence dug up on Powell the previous December by the House Administration Committee, evidence pointing to his mismanagement of the staff and travel funds that were under his control as a representative and as chairman of the Education and Labor Committee. The Celler Committee upheld the charges against Powell and proposed that he be stripped of his twenty-two years of seniority, fined $40,000 and publicly censured in the well of the House—and then seated. For personal, political and racial reasons, 222 members voted to reject this advice, while only 202 voted to follow it. With a compromise route shut off, the House then proceeded to "exclude" Powell from the Ninetieth Congress, or in effect, barred him from membership for the next two years.

To exclude Powell, his opponents needed the approval of only a bare majority of the House. Under the Constitution, had he already been seated, they would have had to win the concurrence of two-thirds of the House in order to "expel" him. Throughout the history of the republic, few have faced either prospect.

A glance at what might be termed the House's "punishment scoreboard" reveals how delicately members tread along paths that lead to their colleagues' doorstep. The record from 1789 through 1974:

Expelled— 3
Excluded— 7
Censured—17

Expulsion, of course, is the severest form of discipline the House is empowered to administer. So warily did they regard the notion of overriding the wishes of the voters that the framers of the Constitution insisted upon the two-thirds vote of concurrence. In line with this thinking, the House established a precedent that a member could be expelled only for misdeeds committed *after* his election. The rationale was that anything done before then would have been considered by the voters, with their verdict handed down at the ballot box. Attesting to the awe with which the House approaches expulsion is the stark statistical fact that of the nearly 9,000 members who served between 1789 and 1975, only three have succumbed to the process. And even supercivil libertarians probably would not quibble with those. All three were ousted in 1861 for joining the Confederacy.

Exclusion is a backdoor method of getting rid of someone, without having to hurdle the constitutional obstacles involved in the expulsion procedure. The word "exclusion" is not mentioned in the Constitution. Its use as a disciplinary tool grew from the constitutional injunction in Article One that the House and Senate "shall be the judge of the elections, returns and qualifications of its own members."

The first exclusions took place in 1867, a year when animosity from the Civil War still lingered strong in the House chamber. Excluded that year were John Young Brown and John D. Young of Kentucky, both of whom had been accused of giving aid to the Confederacy during the conflict that had ended two years before. In 1868 a member-elect from Georgia, John H. Christy, was denied the seat to which he had been elected for the same reason.

Regardless of how one might feel about their activities during the war, the three Southerners had fulfilled the constitutional requirements for admission to the House. But their exclusion had set a precedent and in an establishment like the House, where precedents have the holy standing of Papal pronouncements, it meant that members from other parts of the country now could veto the choice of the electorate in a particular congressional district. The die had been cast.

So it was that someone in 1870 decided exclusion might be a handy way to finally dispose of B.F. Whittemore, a South Carolinian who, it must be said in defense of the House, would have taxed the patience and fairness of a saint. Whittemore had hit upon the clever, though illegal, scheme of picking up some spare change by selling appointments to the military academies. He was caught, but before the House could expel him he resigned his seat. Then, in a dazzling display of nineteenth century chutzpah, Whittemore ran for the seat in the next election, won and presented himself for admission to the House. His former colleagues turned him down by excluding him.

Justified as the House may have been in excluding Whittemore, its action nevertheless chipped away another chunk from the granite rock of representative government. Instead of seating and then expelling him, or referring the case to the government for criminal prosecution, the House strengthened the questionable exclusion precedent set over the Civil War cases. It also prepared the way for the assumption of jurisdiction over a totally new area.

From official misconduct it pushed the exclusion process next into the field of personal behavior. It was not a member who was barred entry this time, but a delegate (which is why George Cannon from the Territory of Utah does not appear on our scoreboard of excluded *members*). But Cannon's exclusion in 1881, for observing the traditional Mormon practice of polygamy, served as another precedent and was tucked away for use at some future date. The opportunity was seventeen years in coming and again the issue was polygamy. Americans were still caught up in lascivious curiosity over a religion that provided a man with a daily choice of women to share his bed. Their fascination sprouted reformers and demagogues and soon Mormons were the target of a national frenzy.

By 1896 Utah and the Church of Jesus Christ of Latter-day Saints had banned polygamy, a move which cleared away the last obstacles toward the territory's achievement of statehood. In 1899, Representative-elect Brigham Roberts, with election certificate in hand, presented himself in Washington for admission to the House. Beating him there was a petition allegedly bearing the names of seven million persons, demanding that he be "cast out." There were plenty of members ready to do the casting, for Roberts was a polygamist. Although he had accepted the decision to discontinue the institution of polygamy, Roberts, member of an eminent Utah family, took the position of many other Mormon adults: he had a moral responsibility to honor his vows to the women he had married (he was said to be living with three at the time) when polygamy was lawful. But what was a position of principle to him constituted scandalous behavior to millions of Americans.

Predictably, Roberts was asked to step aside when the other members of the Fifty-sixth Congress took their oath of office. On December 5, 1899, the House debated his case and the ensuing rhetoric was predictable. It poured forth from such luminaries as Rep. John F. (Honey Fitz) Fitzgerald, grandfather of John F. Kennedy, the nation's first Catholic president, and someone who should have been sensitive to religious bigotry. Fitzgerald described Mormonism as "legalized licentiousness" which threatened liberty and the home. He warned the House: "Every wife, every mother, every daughter in the land is awaiting the action of this House today." Roberts and his handful of defenders took a legalistic high road. Mormonism was not the issue, they declared. The only question was whether Roberts met the constitutional qualification of age, citizenship and inhabitancy. Since he clearly had and since he held a bona fide certificate of election there were no grounds for barring his entry. Finally, and most importantly, he stressed that the seat belonged to the people of Utah. As long as the people respected the specified qualifications they had the right to fill it with whomever they wanted. "I am not begging any favors of the members of this House," Roberts said. "Under shadow of the Constitution of the United States I demand both for myself and for the people of my state the protection that is due me. It is a demand that I make and not a favor that I ask."

Needless to say that was not the day for cold logic, un-yielding principle and an unapologetic assertion of constitutional rights. The House voted 304 to 32 against seating Roberts, pending an investigation by a select committee. The panel returned several weeks later with a recommendation that Roberts be excluded from the Fifty-sixth Congress and on January 26 the House ushered in the twentieth century by excluding Brigham Roberts. The vote was 268 to 50.

The House's next act of exclusion carried it back to the issue of loyalty. The victim this time was Victor Berger, a nationally known American socialist from Milwaukee. Berger ran afoul of his prospective colleagues' sensibilities because of a conviction of sedition he picked up while speaking out against United States involvement in World War I. During appeal of the conviction and prison sentence (handed down by Judge Kennesaw Mountain Landis, the future baseball commissioner), Berger won election to Congress. Twice, in 1919 and 1920, Berger presented himself for admission to the House and twice he was barred, by votes of 311 to 1 and 330 to 6. Finally, in 1923, after his conviction had been reversed on appeal and he had won election again the House relented and seated him.

Nearly fifty years went by before the House found another Berger or Roberts. It was almost as if a period of laissez-faire ethics behavior had set in. Even *attempts* at discipline were minimal.

It wasn't until the advent of Adam Clayton Powell that House members once again saddled up and strung their ropes. The hanging took place almost one hundred years to the day after exclusion claimed its first victim.

The legal battle over Powell's seat consumed hundreds of thousands of words. The precedent-shattering Supreme Court decision in his favor shocked many people, including most members of the House. Yet the issues involved in the case were relatively uncomplicated and while the Court did something no other court had ever done—injected itself into the internal affairs of Congress—in retrospect its decision seems eminently logical and fair.

The first judge to hear the case, George L. Hart, Jr., of the U.S. District Court in Washington, felt it totally inappropriate for judicial review and dismissed it out of hand. So strongly did Hart concur in the House's reasoning that exclusion was none of the court's business that it would be easy for one to imagine him calmly accepting the little letter Byron Rogers wanted to send, and responding with one of his own: "Dear House. I couldn't agree with you more. You are all excused from this silly suit. With best regards to the Senate, I remain sincerely yours, George L. Hart, Jr."

Although somewhat less sweeping, the U.S. Court of Appeals for the District of Columbia also rejected Powell's claim. The principal opinion of the three-judge panel was written by Circuit Court Judge Warren Burger. It was left to the Supreme Court of Earl Warren, Burger's predecessor as Chief Justice of the United States, to furnish Powell with victory.

The Supreme Court cut right through the mountain of argument, citation and interpretation. To the seven members of the Court voting in favor of the Powell position (Potter Stewart was the only dissenter), the conflicting issues were clear and the remedy simple: "Unquestionably Congress has an interest in preserving its institutional integrity, but in most cases that interest can be sufficiently safeguarded by the exercise of its power to punish its members for disorderly behavior and, in extreme cases, to expel a member with the concurrence of two-thirds."

Their reading of what the Constitution's framers intended, and an examination of basic principles of representative government, convinced the seven justices that the Constitution did not grant Congress the power to deny membership by a majority vote. They summed up their view in elegant simplicity with a quote from one of the Constitution's creators, Alexander Hamilton: "The people should choose whom they please to govern them."

The reaction to the Supreme Court's June 16, 1969, decision was immediate. William Nichols, a middle-aged Democrat from Alabama, summed up the feelings held by many of his colleagues toward both the decision and the Warren Court. He declared it was time "to bring the Supreme Court down to earth."

Missouri's Durward Hall, conservative Republican, enunciator of the most pompous syntax heard in Congress in years, spoke openly of defiance. "Either we shall reject the Court's usurpation and sustain the Constitution," said Hall in his richest baritone, "or we shall supinely submit to the spreading judicial tryranny."

And of course someone dragged in Andy Jackson and John Marshall. In this instance, it was Mississippi's William Colmer. But it was left to Lionel Van Deerlin, the man who couldn't bear to serve in Congress with a lawmaker who had been "defiant of the courts of law," to walk away with hypocrisy-of-the-day honors. Van Deerlin didn't come right out and ask the House to ignore the Court's ruling. Instead he regretfully observed that the decision would encourage others to defy the Court legislatively, saying that in fact a majority of the House "almost certainly" would refuse to appropriate the money that the Court had indicated Powell had coming to him in back pay.

As it turned out, Powell himself spared the House and the judiciary the ugly confrontation that had been forecast by Van Deerlin and others. He neglected to follow the legal

avenue the Supreme Court had laid out for him to claim
the $55,000 lost in salary because of his illegal exclusion.
Exactly why is unclear. It seemed to be a combination of
reasons. Herbert Reid, one of his lawyers, felt that by the
time the pay issue had come to a head in the courts Powell
had spiritually, physically, and politically run out of steam.
As usual there was difficulty getting money to pay legal expenses. (Jean Cahn, another one of his attorneys, says the
exclusion case personally cost her $10,000. She also says it
was worth it.) But unlike before, Powell now seemed not
to care how or whether the money was raised.

The Supreme Court victory failed to revive Powell's
political career. Had he been the Powell of old he might
have turned the decision into a springboard in an effort to
propel himself back to the top, though he probably couldn't
have made it. As it was, he didn't even try. After serving
out his exclusion during the Ninetieth Congress,* he ran
in the 1968 election, and of course triumphed. On January
3, 1969, he showed up in the House for the opening day
swearing-in ceremony with the other members elected to
the Ninety-first Congress. Diehard Powell foes made a last
ditch attempt to keep him out, but this time the House,
after slapping him with a $25,000 fine, voted to seat him.
He took his oath and that was almost the last anyone in
Washington saw of Adam Clayton Powell.

Stripped of his chairmanship and seniority, evicted from
his plush Rayburn Building suite to an office in the drab
Longworth Building, Powell lacked the substance or even
image of power, influence and prestige. He was, in short,
just another freshman member. Rather than bear the in-

---

* Powell entered and won the April 1967 election that had been called
to fill the vacancy created by his exclusion. But certain that the House
would again bar him, he never presented himself for admission on the
basis of that victory, thus leaving Harlem unrepresented in the House
during 1967 and 1968.

dignity and the daily reminder of his status, he retreated
to Bimini. There he lived out what were to be his last, painful years, his spiritual despondency deepened by the cancer
that had recently struck. His frequent absences from Washington, his obvious inactivity and his invisibility to the
voters generated complaints and encouraged challengers
back in Harlem. The sad reality was that the people of the
Eighteenth District still had no representation in the
House. In 1970 State Assemblyman Charles Rangel, a
former political associate, took on Powell in the Democratic
Primary and beat him. That rejection by the people of
Harlem apparently shattered Powell even more than the
punishment administered by the House. This one could
not be attributed to racism.

The one-time giant of American and black politics had
had it. In April, 1972, he became gravely ill and was flown
to a Miami hospital. He died there on April 4. A few days
later his ashes were carried aloft by a plane and scattered
over his beloved Bimini.

Adam Clayton Powell had been destroyed. Whether he
destroyed himself or whether the House destroyed him, and
did so because he was black, can be argued over and over.
My own view is that those who set in motion the events that
led to his destruction were not out to crush a black political
figure who had amassed too much power, as Powell charged
and as some of his supporters believe. But I think it is safe
to say that in the fight to save his seat, as opposed to the
battle over his chairmanship, Powell's race defeated him.

On the critical 222 to 202 vote rejecting the Celler Committee proposal only six southerners—five Texans and

Majority Whip Hale Boggs—stuck with Powell. The House contained many more southerners than that who wanted to be fairminded whenever it was either possible or desirable. Andrew Jacobs, a member of the Celler Committee, recalled later in his book, *The Powell Affair: Freedom Minus One:*

"More members of Congress than the twenty by which the Select Committee recommendation was rejected, approached me afterward to say privately they thought the committee's recommendations were right, but that a vote for seating would have meant their own unseating in the next election. . . .

"I cannot say exactly how many racially prejudiced whites sit as members of the United States House of Representatives. Certainly, they are a minority. But from personal observation, I should not be surprised that the number exceeded the twenty by which the Select Committee recommendation was voted down in the Ninetieth Congress. The racially prejudiced would never be permitted to sit as jurors in the case of a black litigant. Nonetheless, not one disqualified himself in the vote on the Select Committee recommendation."

Many northerners voted against Powell. I don't think it was racism that motivated most of them. Rather, they allowed Powell's outrageous behavior and the public hysteria it provoked to blind them to their constitutional duty. *The New York Times,* for example, did its part to fan the flames. The day after Van Deerlin announced his plans to exclude Powell, *The Times* jumped into the fray with an enthusiastic editorial of support. Not only did *The Times,* which had been critical of Powell for years, agree that he should not be allowed to sit in the House while court judgments were hanging over him, but it applauded the clever device Van Deerlin had come up with to accomplish the objective. "This is a sensible tactic," it said in its December 2, 1966, editorial. "Exclusion, which requires merely a majority vote, is simpler and easier to obtain than expulsion, which requires a two-thirds vote."

On March 2, however, the day *after* Powell had been ousted, *The Times* observed that the House had "acted hastily and unwisely in excluding him at this time" (and in following the advice of its December 2 editorial). The preferable course, thought *The Times,* would have been to keep Powell in limbo, neither in nor out of the House, until he had resolved his difficulties with the law. When the Supreme Court ruled in 1969 that the exclusion of Powell had been unconstitutional, *The Times* hailed the decision as the correct one.

What *The Times* had failed to realize at the outset was that once any concession was made on Powell's claim to his seat, the battle was over. Unless the public and the House could be persuaded that the voters of Harlem were the ones who should decide who represents them, no partial or temporary seating plan would still the outcry for Powell's scalp. Like the socialist Berger and the Mormon Roberts before him, the people wanted Powell out and they wanted him out quickly.

Then there were many members in 1967 who knew better but who yielded to the passion of the day when it came to dealing with Adam Clayton Powell. The list of those who voted to reject the Celler Committee's seat-and-punish plan includes the names of members who were considered judicious and reasoned. Many more such congressmen, including then Majority Leader Carl Albert, and GOP Conference Chairman John Anderson, voted to admit Powell but then voted to exclude him after all had been lost and it was obvious he was not going to be seated. The

House had rejected the "seat"; half of the Celler Committee's seat-and-punish plan and the people were demanding that Powell be punished. These lawmakers, realizing there was nothing more they could do for him, felt they had no choice politically but to climb on the exclusion bandwagon. One of those who did and later regretted it was Charles Whalen, a thoughtful Republican from Dayton, Ohio. Even though it would not have gotten Powell into the House, Whalen wishes he had stuck with Powell to the end and voted against the final exclusion resolution.

"The issue was, should Powell go scot-free or should he be excluded," Whalen recalls. "The middle ground had been completely wiped out. At that time I said to myself I can't let him off completely. Well, I was just wrong on it. I have several votes that I would like to have back and that's one of them. It troubled me afterwards for a long time. I agreed with the Supreme Court decision. In 1969 I tried to redeem myself by voting to admit Powell. But in 1967 I have to castigate myself. I was swept up with the emotion of the time."

Yet there is still another dimension to be considered. The Powell affair, as has no other issue in years, reflected the insular mentality that afflicts the House and many of its members. It is *their* House, *their* third of the government, *their* club, and like any self-respecting club it is *their* prerogative, nay their obligation, to bring to heel those members who do not live up to the fellowship's proclaimed standards. It is none of the Court's business. He broke *our* rules; he's *our* responsibility. Consequently, men like Durward Hall, men who daily put long, hard hours of work into seeing that the House performs up to snuff, looked upon Powell as someone who had stained the reputation of the House and had to be punished. To Hall, the House was not so much a collection of people's representatives as an association, which men and women were privileged to belong to and in which they continually would have to earn the right to remain. The voters of Harlem would have to elect someone else, that's all there was to it. And if they persisted in sending back Powell, well then they would have brought upon themselves the penalty of nonrepresentation.

8

Hobgoblins in Flight

FORCE A HOUSE member to reverse a position or backtrack on something he has said and nine times out of ten he'll tell you that "consistency is the hobgoblin of little minds." It's a popular phrase during floor debates. Emerson wrote that "foolish" consistency was the hobgoblin, but that weakens the point so most members omit the modifier.

Consistency is not one of the House's strong points. Hypocrisy is. Much self-defeating, time-consuming nonsense takes place in the House that cannot be laughed off by deprecating consistency. It boils down to unvarnished hypocrisy.

At the time that the House was excluding Adam Clayton Powell from membership, his former colleagues were publicly vowing that henceforth the House would be made safe for decent men and women. A code of ethics was adopted, a limited financial disclosure system was put into effect, and an Ethics Committee was created to monitor the representatives' official conduct.

Since 1967, when Powell was ousted and the ethics machinery was assembled, House members have been as loose if not looser in their behavior than they were before. That isn't to say that they've established themselves as a pack of reprobates. The proportion of wrongdoers among them is probably the same as that among other professions. Congressmen make inviting targets in the press because they are often sanctimonious about what others' conduct ought to be and are hypocritical about their own. To have heard the expressions of piety sounded during the Powell proceedings, one would have thought the House was about to turn into a monastery.

Since then at least half a dozen members and ex-members have been convicted for crimes committed while sitting in Congress. Several others have been indicted and, while indictment is not proof of a crime, it should also be pointed out that a number of other lawmakers apparently were eligible for indictment but were spared prosecution by a politically motivated attorney-general, John Mitchell.

Meanwhile, countless members have run afoul of Washington area police over traffic incidents (for which they rarely face charges) after visits to the city's public or private watering holes. Speaker Carl Albert made the network news when his car careened off a parked vehicle following a stop-off at the Zebra Room. Wilbur Mills kept headline writers across the country busy with his succession of explanations of the bon voyage party he hosted, first at the Junkanoo Restaurant and then at the Tidal Basin. Many similar incidents, involving lesser known members, go unrecorded by the national media.

During the same period, the media has carried dozens of allegations of wrongdoing on the part of members, including some who served on the Ethics Committee. The Ethics Committee has adroitly managed to come up with reasons for looking the other way in each and every instance. If the case involved an intoxicated member, ripping up part of Georgetown one night, well, that's the kind of "personal" conduct that the creators of the committee promised the House it wouldn't investigate. And if the charge dealt with something more serious, like a kickback scheme that the member has arranged with his employees, well, that would constitute a criminal act and that's a job for the Justice Department.

A few embarrassments surfaced that even the Ethics Committee couldn't avoid. Like the so-called "ghost voting" scandal in which members, before the installation of the electronic voting system, arranged for tally clerks to record them as present on quorum calls when in fact they were out of town. The scheme bolstered their attendance record. Although there was clear-cut proof that some members were active participants, the Ethics Committee concluded that it was the fault of sloppy employees and closed the books on the case by firing one of them.

Another made-to-order case arose when two of my colleagues at UPI—Frank Eleazer and Roy McGhee—discovered that the Ford Motor Company was leasing Lincoln Continentals to key representatives and senators for $750 a year, about a fifth of what it would cost ordinary citizens. The practice was a clear violation of the ethics code. Their stories prompted John Stennis, chairman of the Senate Ethics Committee, to order an immediate halt to the practice on his side of the Capitol. Meanwhile, chairman Melvin Price and the House Ethics Committee took the matter under study, wrestled with it and did nothing. Finally, Ford itself, unhappy with the damaging publicity, called in the cars. At that point, the House committee announced that the issue was moot.

The Ethics Committee's sole purpose since its inception

has been to serve as the repository of the financial disclosure statements members are required to file. The same function could be just as easily handled by the Clerk of the House.

Sexual misconduct is not among the usual allegations leveled against members. Occasionally an incident surfaces, such as in 1967 when an admitted call girl testified at a pandering trial in Alexandria, Virginia, that among her interstate clients was one "Al O'Konski" in the Rayburn Office Building. O'Konski, a likable reprobate who held a minimum regard for serious legislative inquiry and hard work, laughed off the charge and indeed used it to his advantage in winning reelection. He convinced his northern Wisconsin constituents that the heart attack he had suffered a few months before had not incapacitated him. Coincidentally, the call girl gave her testimony on April 13, 1967, the same day that O'Konski joined 399 colleagues in unanimously voting to establish the Ethics Committee.

Though formal allegations of sexual hijinks are few, now and then there are whispers and stories of women put through difficult times. Here is the account of one young woman who went up to the House looking for a job:

"We were sitting around chatting and he asked me if I was on the pill, if I was a bed hopper. He asked me where I got my 'sugar.' I asked him what he meant and he smiled. He slid into it so easily. I was really taken off guard. I'm not apt to react really fast anyway. I kept thinking I was overreacting but it got to the point where all I wanted to do was get out the door and I wasn't sure I was going to be able to do that. His secretary had left at 4:30 or 5:00 and I began to wonder if I was even going to get out. His language was pretty gross. Then he says, 'How liberated are you?' And I asked 'What do you mean by that?' So he comes over and reaches behind me, feels my back and sees I wasn't wearing a bra. So he decided I was pretty liberated. He started grabbing at my breasts and making all kinds of passes, trying to kiss me and smother me and everything else. The biggest thing in my mind was just to get out.

"Afterwards I didn't talk about it. I was so embarrassed about the way I reacted. That I just didn't kick him or something. I finally decided I should start talking about it because other people may be going through the same thing. If they give him the right answers, maybe they end up with a job."

Hypocrisy and lack of consistency are found in the House's public demeanor as well as in members' private lives.

The House, as members are fond of saying in speeches, belongs to the American people. You wouldn't know it from the way the House treats the people who visit it.

Signs abound everywhere ordering tourists away. They and other nonmembers are ordered away from certain elevators and subway cars. They are ordered away from congressional parking lots and garages. They are ordered away from the cafeterias during the prime lunch hours, and once inside they are ordered not to take any pictures. (A restriction imposed by Administration Committee Chairman Wayne Hays after some employees staged a well-publicized "bag-in" protest over increased prices.)

Visitors are permitted in the House galleries but they are not allowed to take notes. Nor is the tourist or uninitiated given any help—such as a brochure—to explain the strange parliamentary terms he hears and the often confusing proceedings that unfold below him.

Outsiders are able to sit in on open hearings. But if the sessions are popular the hearing rooms will quickly fill with staff, witnesses and accompanying officials, news personnel, friends and relatives of the members, and early arrivals. There's little room for anyone else, like the tourist who drops by. It could have been otherwise, but the congressional creators of the Rayburn Building designed the rooms in a way that guaranteed wasted space to serve as a grand backdrop for members—such as two-story ceilings—and relatively little space for spectators.

You don't have to hang around the House very long to realize that most members, at least unconsciously, think of the place as theirs. To some extent they regard it as an enclave within the United States, part of the government and eligible at demand for its protection, but not necessarily subject to the laws of the land.

In spring 1974 the Environmental Protection Agency outlined a long-range plan that would enable the Washington metropolitan area to achieve the clean air goals established by Congress. As it did with many other urban centers, the EPA wanted to restrict private automobile travel into the city and proposed prohibitive parking surcharges as a way of doing it.

Wayne Hays took it upon himself to voice the House reaction: if anybody from the city dared set foot in a House garage and tried to collect a parking tax from congressmen or employees he would have them thrown out by the Capitol police. It was the usual Hays bluster and headline grabbing, and as it turned out, academic. The plan was shelved for other reasons. But the interesting thing is that no one in the House bothered to dispel the image Hays was on the way to creating, namely that congressmen were above enduring the hardships and inconveniences that the rest of us were saddled with. The example carried two ironies. It was Congress which had directed EPA to propose the kind of plan that it did. And if the people who worked on Capitol Hill did eventually pay a parking tax they'd still be way ahead of most of us. Their parking is free, a gift from the taxpayers.

Sometimes freeloading and convenience-seeking by members extends beyond the Capitol grounds. A few years ago the Federal Aviation Administration decided that Washington National Airport was becoming dangerously overcrowded. The agency figured the best way to solve the problem was to shift part of the load to Dulles International Airport, the big new terminal in the Virginia countryside. Officials decreed that cities more than 500 miles from Washington would be serviced through Dulles.

Although Dulles had plenty of room, it was also located almost an hour away from the Capitol. National, on the other hand, was just across the Potomac and barely fifteen minutes from the Capitol. Members from districts outside the 500-mile radius howled. The loudest screams came from those flying from Chicago. The FAA caved in and the radius was extended to encompass Chicago.

Today, National Airport is one of the most congested airports in the country—for pilots, airport personnel and ordinary travelers. Getting to the airport with an automobile is a handwringing experience. Parking within walking distance from the terminal is becoming the exception. Parking, however, is not a problem for members of Congress. Lawmakers, with Supreme Court justices and diplomats, enjoy reserved spaces a few yards from the terminal.

The House's attitude toward Vietnam veterans has been something just short of a national disgrace, though largely an unnoticed one. In 1974, when the full extent of the country's neglect toward the veterans became known and felt, the House joined the chorus criticizing the Veterans Administration and its administrator, Donald E. Johnson. As much as that criticism may have been warranted, the House should have been one of the last to be voicing it. The principal reason for the dismal plight of the veterans was the niggardly sums of money spent on them, niggardly in comparison with that spent on World War II and Korean War vets. Congress had opportunity to appropriate hundreds of millions more than it did. Neither the House nor the Senate had to accept the pitiful level of subsistence proposed for the GI Bill by the administration. No one in the House—including the Veterans Affairs Committee—took as much interest in the veterans as the Armed Services Committee did in the active GIs. When Robert McNamara and Lyndon Johnson sent up a pay hike for servicemen, Mendel Rivers dismissed it as inadequate and pushed through a bill that doubled the raise. Neither the administration nor the president dared to veto it. No similar efforts were made with veterans' benefits until 1974.

For nine years the House whooped along the war in Vietnam, approving every appropriation request that came its way. Usually defenders of Indochina policy bellowed that a refusal to go along with the administration would amount to a betrayal of the troops, to a pulling the rug from under the boys, as some liked to put it. Interestingly, they seemed less disturbed about sending the boys over there. Perhaps one reason was that the boys rarely came from their families and hardly ever from their social and economic classes.

In 1967 the House Armed Services Committee rejected the Johnson administration's plans for eliminating college student deferments and placing the draft on a lottery basis. Instead, the committee went beyond the old discretionary policy of granting college deferments and ordered the president to give a four-year deferment to any student who one way or the other could manage to stay in college. It contended that the national interest required an uninterrupted flow of college graduates and that the system of discretionary deferments was often inequitable. The House, of course, went along and in conference the Senate Armed Services Committee was persuaded to buy the plan. The net result was that over the next four years anybody who could afford to get into a college and stay there was excused from fighting. The years 1967 to 1971 also happened to be the heaviest casualty years of the war, in which more than 35,000 Americans died in combat and more than 125,000 were wounded.

The brunt of the casualties was borne by lower-middle-class and poor youths, those bright enough to pass army aptitude tests but not smart or rich enough to handle college. Yet, congressmen from big cities and small towns, representing neighborhoods from which those youths were drawn, blandly and blindly went along with the Armed Services Committee's draft plan and the Johnson and Nixon administrations' war plans. Neither in politics nor in the media was the point hammered home that it was their constituents who were making up most of the casualties.

Statistics detailing the impact on members' families by the deferment action are not available. The closest are the figures compiled in 1970 by *Congressional Quarterly*— while students were eligible for but not guaranteed a deferment. CQ found that between 1965 and 1970 only one out of seven members of Congress could claim a son or grandson who had served in the armed forces since the United States became deeply involved in Vietnam combat operations. Of the 234 draft eligible sons, 118—or just about 50 percent—received deferments. Twenty-six of the remainder served in Vietnam and 49 others served in the military but not in Vietnam. Only one member, Rep.

Clarence Long, Democrat from Maryland, had a son who was wounded in Vietnam. He turned against the war with the invasion of Cambodia and became a prominent sponsor of end-the-war amendments.

None of the senior members of the Armed Services Committee in 1971—the men who made the crucial decisions about the draft—had sons that served in Vietnam. Few if any had boys going into the military during this period.

No major drive was ever launched in the House to upgrade the GI bill so that Vietnam veterans could receive the same educational benefits as World War II and Korean veterans. Nor did any House committee ever investigate what was being done for the six million refugees that Sen. Edward Kennedy's subcommittee estimated had been created by the war. Nor did any committee ever bother to find out why so little government money was going into medical care for the hundreds of thousands of South Vietnamese who were seriously wounded in the war. A great deal of rhetoric was heard, however, about keeping U.S. forces in South Vietnam to protect it from a communist bloodbath.

The House is not an equal opportunity employer. That in itself is ironic. In 1964 the House and Senate mandated that practically everybody else in the country must hire, promote and otherwise employ people without regard to race, color, national origin, and sex. Since 1964, federal agencies and commissions, the courts, corporations, labor unions, universities and local governments have been wrestling with the problems and challenges posed by that legislative decision.

Not much wrestling has been going on at the House. Congress conveniently exempted itself from the provisions of the Civil Rights Act. That omission had the effect of denying to 17,500 employees—and countless prospective employees—the remedies to job discrimination that the rest of us can seek at the Equal Employment Opportunity Commission and the courts. The results are what you might expect. The House's professional echelons are overwhelmingly white and male. Its lower ranks are predominantly black and female.

More than 10,000 people worked for the House in the summer of 1974. Hard statistics on the makeup of that labor force are impossible to come by. Most of the employers were not required to keep figures and they didn't. But from personal observation and scanning of available records some approximations can be deduced.

Slightly more than 1,000 people worked for the twenty-two permanent House committees in 1974. The District of Columbia Committee was filled with black and female professionals. That wasn't surprising; it was chaired by black Rep. Charles Diggs. Serving as the professional staff consultant to the African affairs subcommittee at Foreign Affairs was a black woman lawyer. Diggs, who also heads that subcommittee, found her at the State Department where she was attached to the African desk. The Education and Labor Committee still contains a few holdover black professionals from the days of Adam Clayton Powell. And that's it. There are no black professionals to be found on any of the other nineteen committees.

Women weren't doing much better. Some of the lesser committees, particularly if they were chaired by a woman, show the impact that a woman can produce when she takes over. But the major committees, such as Ways and Means, Armed Services, Banking and Currency, Government Operations, Commerce and Judiciary, could not claim a single female professional. The Appropriations Committee, with a staff of about seventy-five, had one woman in a professional position, a staff assistant to the Republican members.

The Offices of the Clerk, the Sergeant at Arms, and the Architect of the Capitol employed about 2,000 people. Only a handful of supervisory positions were filled by women or members of minority groups.

The bulk of the House labor force worked for the 435 members, each entitled to sixteen employees. Progress here is mixed. Black secretaries began showing up in offices, including those of southern white lawmakers who never before had a Negro on the staff. Women were moving up from other than secretarial positions to jobs as legislative or press aides and sometimes as administrative assistants. But aside from black members, it was rare to see a black male working in a congressman's office. And the emergence of an activist branch of the National Women's Political Caucus among employees attested to the fact that female employees were anything but satisfied with their condition. They were able to cite examples of gross inequities between the pay of men and women doing the same work. And too often it is only the female applicant for the professional job who is asked if she can type.

The absence of blacks and women in professional posts in the House could not be swept aside with the explanation that qualified people from these groups were not available. Government agencies in Washington, responding to pressure from above and from the outside have placed thousands of blacks and women in posts that until a few years ago were filled almost exclusively by white males.

As far as I know, no civil rights or women's group has ever proposed that congressmen be required to initiate affirmative action hiring programs for their personal staffs.

The need to establish special personal and political relationships between a member and his aides would argue in
favor of giving the legislator a free hand in deciding who
to hire. But that doesn't mean he should be permitted to
state religious, racial or sexual preferences when he puts
in a request for a secretary to the Placement Office of the
Joint Committee on Congressional Operations. Yet, about
a score of lawmakers were doing just that, until 1974 when
a story by Francie Barnard of the Fort Worth, Texas,
Star-Telegram brought the practice to a halt. What was
going on would have been a gross violation of the law had
it taken place in private industry, state or local government,
or even the executive branch of the federal government.
But Congress excluded itself from the Civil Rights Act,
just as it had excluded itself from various labor and safety
laws and the Freedom of Information Act.

You'll find plenty of blacks working in the House restaurant and cafeterias. A few have recently advanced to
positions such as cashier and baker, but most of the supervisory and administrative jobs are still filled by whites. For
the majority of employees, pay is low, job security is poor,
benefits are marginal and status is for others. The middle-
aged women who serve the cafeteria's customers are listed
in pay records as "counter girls." Most of them make less
money than sixteen-year-old pages. During recesses and
holidays the waiters (all of whom are black) and other dining room and kitchen personnel are laid off without pay.

When Wayne Hays became chairman of the Administration Committee he took over control of the House's food
operations and set out to erase its perennial deficit. One of
his first moves was to reduce the work day—and thus the
salaries—of restaurant and cafeteria employees. Hays
claimed it was a necesary budget cutting step. Yet as part of
a log-rolling arrangement with another member, Hays and

his Administration Committee approved an annual $30,000 a year appropriation to staff something called the House Restaurant Committee, a panel that hasn't held a hearing in three years and has no plans to hear any in the next three. Hays permitted its continuation as a friendly gesture to its chairman, John Kluczynski of Chicago. The money spent on the committee was totally wasted. It could have been applied to the deficit of the restaurant, or to much needed raises for the people working there.

With great fanfare and amidst waves of self-congratulation, Congress in 1966 passed the Freedom of Information Act. The law states in beautifully simple English that "any person" has the right to see most government records. Congress, however, excluded itself from the act. Thus, the record of openness on Capitol Hill is spotty. It depends on the willingness of members and committees to live the spirit of the Freedom of Information Act.

In many ways the House can stir a fresh breeze into a Washington debate. Information can be procured from the Armed Services Committee that could never be pried out of the Pentagon. And since the reforms of 1971, many previously closed legislative sessions are open to public view.

But partly canceling out those credits, is the closing up of sources of information about the House's internal operations, how the House spends the hundreds of millions of dollars a year that the taxpayers provide, what the House does with the thousands of people it employs. The General Accounting Office, at the request of House leaders and officials, runs audits on specific operations and projects. But the audits, unlike GAO investigations of executive branch

operations, are rarely made public. If scandal has been uncovered, we are not necessarily going to find out.

The ascension of Wayne Hays to the chairmanship of the
Administration Committee has further restricted the flow
of information about the House in recent years. Hays abol-
ished a longstanding procedure by which newsmen could
examine current payroll records. Now they can find out
who's on the payroll only by reading the semiannual *Clerk's
Report,* a document that is published a month or two after
the close of a six-month period. If a congressman has hired
a political crony during the election campaign, a reporter
won't find out till three or four months after the election
is over.

Until 1974, committees were required by law to file an
nually in the *Congressional Record* relatively complete
junketing records on which members and staff traveled
abroad at government expense, where they went and how
much they spent. The House alone usually racked up more
than half a million dollars a year in cash travel costs, not to
mention the expenses borne by the State Department and
Pentagon transporting and tending to members and sometimes their wives.

In the fall of 1973, Hays quietly attached to an unrelated
bill an amendment ending the requirement that the material be published in the *Congressional Record*. It was replaced by a provision directing committees to provide a
limited amount of travel information to anyone who asked.
Congressional Quarterly, which discovered the Hays ploy,
tried and found out that information there ranged from in-
complete to nonexistent. Hays claimed "there was no desire
on anyone's part to cover up anything," but he added:

"We decided we weren't going to spend eight or nine
thousand dollars (in printing costs) to let you guys do your

stories on congressional travel." What Hays did not add was that the stories invariably stirred up public outrage at the excesses in congressional travel.

Fortunately, *CQ*'s story set loose a barrage of editorials throughout the country. As a result, some enlightened lawmakers inserted into another bill an amendment modifying the repeal. Still missing was the requirement that the junketing figures be printed in the *Congressional Record*. But at least they would be filed, for public viewing, with the clerk of the House and the secretary of the Senate.

Probably the longest standing and most idiotic curtailment of information by the House can be found in the galleries in the House chamber. There spectators are prohibited from writing. A citizen interested in what his representative is doing or saying cannot jot down notes. Nor can a scholar doing research. Nor can a freelance writer. Nor can correspondents with publications that do not meet criteria for accreditation at the press galleries. The restriction is more than incidental. Ninety percent of what is said on the House floor, for a variety of reasons, is not reported in the press. What appears in the *Congressional Record* may be shamefully altered. In this day of instant recording and copying devices historians find themselves in the position of being unable to know with certainty what was said on the floor of the House.

A further irony is that no one is sure why the rule exists or when it was adopted. Nor is anyone in a position to do so willing to change it.

The House at War

A few minutes after noon on a sunny day in early March, not long after Tet Offensive and My Lai, a stream of limousines produced a minor traffic jam in front of the Rayburn Office Building. The limousines were carrying and depositing dozens of senior government officials, high ranking military officers, politicians and defense industry executives. They had come to pay homage to and accept the hospitality of Mendel Rivers at his annual "quail and she-crab" luncheon for his good friend, Speaker John McCormack. The presence of Vice-President Hubert Humphrey, Defense Secretary Clark Clifford, other cabinet officers and all available members of the Joint Chiefs of Staff said all that had to be said about the stature of the host.

Rivers and McCormack made much of their friendship, describing themselves as the only members of a two-man political party known as the "McCormacrats." They made a distinctive pair. The elderly McCormack was tall, gaunt and ashen faced. He invariably wore a black suit, its jacket pockets sagging with messages and assorted slips of paper. He looked and sounded like a struggling South Boston undertaker. Rivers, about fifteen years younger, stood straight and sturdy. His striking feature was a mane of flowing white hair that fell below his collar, a twentieth century rendition of his South Carolina predecessor, John C. Calhoun.

Although McCormack voted traditional northern big city liberalism on welfare and civil rights issues while Rivers generally, though not always, followed the southern conservative pattern, the two shared a deep loyalty to the Democratic party, a common affection for the House and, most significantly, an abiding conviction that a militarily strong and aggressive America was the country's best guarantee of peace.

McCormack, of course, did not claim to know as much about military matters as Rivers, who spent nearly thirty years on the Armed Services Committee and served as its chairman from 1965 until his death on December 28, 1970. So when Pentagon critics would give Mendel a bit of a hard time during debate over a weapons system, his friend John McCormack would rise and help him out. McCormack would concede that he didn't know much about the weapon in question. But two things he did know. One was that when it came to matters of defense, it paid "to err on the side of strength." The lessons of the 1930s should have made that plain to anyone. The other thing he knew was that when it came to technical military matters he'd follow the advice of experts like Mendel Rivers. And with that scores of northern Democrats, who easily could have voted the other way, would march up the aisle with Rivers and McCormack in support of the Pentagon.

The result was that a few projects that should have been killed—such as the army's Cheyenne Helicopter—were kept alive. (The cost and the performance of the Cheyenne got to be enough of an embarrassment so that in 1972, four years and several hundred million dollars after McCormack helped foil an effort to halt it, the army canceled the program.)

It wasn't only questionable weapons systems that the House gave its blessing to. The willingness of rank-and-file Democrats to go along with McCormack who went along with Rivers, the proclivity of conservative Republicans to "stand up to the communists," all primed the House for a longstanding military adventure. The opportunity came in the form of Vietnam. Once committed, the House hung on tenaciously to Vietnam and became one of the last institutions in the country to let go. It stuck with the war well beyond the point where the Senate was ready to let go, and its unbending stand meant that Americans fought there a year-and-a-half longer than they might have otherwise.

🏴

One of the most powerful men in the House during the 1960s was Russell Blandford. You won't find Blandford's name on any list of members for the period. He was an employee of the House, or to be more specific, chief counsel to the House Armed Services Committee. To be still more specific, Blandford served as the blocking back, confidant, adviser and alter ego of L. Mendel Rivers, the panel's chairman. Rivers delegated enormous chunks of authority to his short, burly aide during the five years that the South Carolinian reigned as chairman of the committee, so much authority that most of those at the Pentagon—and even a few members of Congress—jumped to the deep, booming voice of Russ Blandford as if it were that of Mendel Rivers.

Generals and admirals caught hell if they failed to carry out a committee order to his satisfaction, high civilian officials endured his grilling at hearings, lobbyists eagerly sought him out for lunch and committee members had to get his okay before they could go off on a junket.

In effect, he was Rivers's chief of staff and he boasted ideal qualifications for the job. With the exception of World War II service in the marines, virtually his entire career was spent on the staff of the committee. He loved the military, and in fact refused to see any awkwardness in retaining his Marine Corps reserve commission, or accepting a final promotion to brigadier general while supposedly keeping a check on the military for Congress. But he also appreciated intellect and felt confident enough of his own to reach firm conclusions on an array of global and national issues, conclusions which he would pass on to Rivers.

The two of them would meet for breakfast at 6:45 A.M. (Rivers was an insomniac) and map plans for the committee's next adventure or devise tactics for a current battle. In so doing, they would set in motion the chain of thinking that would culminate in committee decisions—to go along with, or oppose a critical administration proposal on the draft; to approve or disapprove development of a fullblown antiballistic missile system; how to block McNamara from merging the army reserves into the National Guard or how to force a reluctant Laird to spend millions Congress appropriated for unwanted navy ships.

It wasn't all that hard to get the committee together on an issue. The overwhelming majority were like-minded— in favor of a strong defense—but sometimes they needed a cue, sometimes they had to be coaxed into following a particular strategy. A committee decision, in turn, was automatically followed on the floor of the House. And in conference, negotiators from the Senate Armed Services Committee usually deferred to the House delegation when a strongly pro-Pentagon House bill had to be reconciled with a more modest Senate measure.

So the early morning conversations in the House cafeteria or Rivers's office carried special significance. What the two men decided did not necessarily always evolve into national policy, but it occasionally did and in any event the men in the Pentagon and the White House had to confront and deal with the Armed Services Committee positions, often wrapping them into the decisions that were finally reached. Keeping this in mind, Blandford's influence on Rivers cannot be underestimated. In spite of his flamboyance, Rivers displayed traces of inner insecurity, both intellectual and psychological. Blandford, on the other hand, seemed supremely sure of himself. His ability to clearly articulate lofty concepts while spinning off supporting facts and figures must have impressed Rivers, convincing him that Blandford was solid and dependable, a man whose advice could be taken with little risk.

When Rivers died, Blandford stayed on with the new chairman, Hébert, but he was having health problems, and in 1972 he retired at the age of 54. After several months of rest and treatment he felt well enough to open an office as a consultant. Not surprisingly, he quickly landed a few well-heeled, corporate clients who figured they could benefit from Russ Blandford's knowledge of, feel for and contacts in military and legislative affairs.

One day in late 1972, ensconced in a high rise just across the Potomac in Rosslyn, Virginia, Blandford recalled his days with Rivers. He also spoke about America's postwar foreign policy.

"Mendel became a superhawk quickly. His favorite expression was 'there are hawks, doves and capons.'"

Yet Rivers, as far as Blandford knows, never marched down to the White House and told Lyndon Johnson that his administration's limited war aims wouldn't work; that he ought to be blockading and bombing.

"Just between you and me, he didn't get along that well with the president at that time. They were not close friends."

Blandford never had any doubts about what was happening in Southeast Asia.

"Only history will prove whether we were right or wrong to go into Vietnam. But personally I knew we were going to get into a mess and said so and was quite convinced we were going to rue the day we ever went in there unless we went in with the idea of winning a military victory.

"I believed in the domino theory and still do. I don't think Vietnam is the target, I always felt Thailand was the basic target, and after that Malaysia and eventually Indonesia. These are the great raw material resource areas. The objectives of the communists, the people who had been supplying North Vietnam—Russia or China or both—had a bigger goal in mind (than South Vietnam)."

It was during the quiet, fresh hours of the early morning that Rivers and Blandford talked—about Vietnam, about the C-5a, about draft card burners and lots of other subjects that might or might not come before the committee. Most of the time the discussions were pleasant chats between two strong-minded friends who viewed the world through similar prisms. But not always.

"We had some battles between us that people wouldn't believe. One morning the swearing and shouting got so loud that a policeman from down the hall looked in to see if there was a fight going on. This was the kind of language Mendel understood. He liked a good argument. If he felt people were going to knuckle under him he'd run rough-shod over them. One time we ended up really shouting at each other and he stood up with this damn Derringer in his hand, playing with it, not literally pointing it at me. But it always made me nervous. He always had it on his desk in the morning, loaded, because he got here so damn early. I think the only man he ever would have used it on, without any hesitation, was Drew Pearson. Anyway, some minor thing built up into a first class argument and I told him where to go and all of a sudden he stood up and put his arm around me and with tears in his eyes he said, 'You and I are too close to each other to fight like this.' He said, 'You think like I do and I depend on you more than you realize. I have to have someone like you around to tell me when you think I'm wrong.' I had opportunities to move over to Defense as an assistant secretary but he just didn't want me to go . . . ."

On Rivers's drinking: "The stories about it bothered him to no end. Not so much that he resented it, as it affected him. But he used to say to me—and this is why he hated Pearson so much, because Pearson repeated the same thing over and over again—'I've got grandchildren reading this,' he'd tell me. 'Can you imagine what the kids they go to school with are going to say. I'm their grandfather.' This is what really bothered him. And his children. He was worried what Marian and Peg and Mendel Junior were thinking about. . . .

"His drinking episodes were much more exaggerated than they should have been. He was not an 'alcoholic' as we understand the word. He was just one of those unfortunate guys who after a couple of drinks, he was gone. He was just a person who should never touch alcohol, period. It was remarkable how he would stay away from alcohol after he was chairman, absolutely remarkable. It was a tremendous example of restraint. I was so proud of that guy."

But unfortunately there were times when restraint broke down.

"When he got off on one of those episodes it was usually at a party and some guy, a 'well wisher,' who would say, 'I'll get you a ginger ale' and then he'd doctor it with bourbon. I saw this happen when they had a party for me at the University Club when I got the Rockefeller Award. Some joker came over and said, 'Let me get you something cold to drink' and the chairman had had a ginger ale. That's all he drank. And this guy came back with the drink. I saw the chairman raise the glass to his lips, taste it and then gulp it right down. He didn't gulp down ginger ale that way. He gulped this thing down, and boy, that was it. He was gone for about ten days."

The powerful chief counsel for the powerful chairman of the powerful committee: "I guess I have to admit, it frightened me on occasion that he gave me a great deal of responsibility, a great deal of responsibility that a staff member should not have. I know this may sound strange but I don't think staff members should have this much authority. For example, any time a member of the committee wanted to go on a trip some place, investigate something or other, he required them to come and see me. Certain places he wouldn't let them go. They had to have a legitimate reason to travel and they had to have an itinerary that indicated they were going to be on committee business. And he made them all come down and clear it with me. Well, that put me in a pretty awkward position, as you can well imagine. Because I knew what he wanted and there were occasions when I had to say, 'You can't go, there's no legitimate reason.' And they thought I had made the decision. And they were right. But it was a duty imposed on me. And they started taking me apart in the newspaper as a potentate and all that sort of thing. In that sense of the word, I guess I was. I had a lot more responsibility than I really wanted.

"Oh sure, I thoroughly enjoyed it. But at the same time it frightened me. Here, I thought are nonelected people (staff members), responsible only to the chairman and to the members of the committee. You don't respond to the people. It literally would frighten me. I used to go home and tell my wife that there are things I shouldn't be doing. And if the chairman was away he'd turn over running of the operation to me.

"I knew there was some resentment among the members. I'm just amazed they were as kind as they were. Most of them, I think not all of them, recognized that I didn't seek this. It made me a pretty nervous guy, simply because I have so much respect for the legislative process. If it ever breaks down the country's gone."

Ernest Fitzgerald is another noncongressman who knows a good deal about Congress. He is the air force management expert who angered his superiors and got himself fired because he told a congressional committee that the C-5a transport program would cost $2 billion more than the Pentagon was admitting. What is less known about Fitzgerald is that he is a true southern populist (he's from Alabama) and, like Harry Truman's, his beliefs are fashioned from his own observations and reading of history. He doesn't drink from the fountain of conventional wisdom.

One day in late 1972, while he was fighting to get his air force job back (a fight he won) and working part time for Sen. William Proxmire, his principal congressional champion, he sat down with me in the Senate cafeteria. It was

well past lunch hour and there, amidst the clatter of workers cleaning up, he talked about congressmen, military
men, defense firms and the Vietnam War.

I asked him about the familiar lament that Congress was
short on the necessary information and expertise to challenge the Pentagon on national security issues.

"That's a cop-out. We got that repeatedly on the C-5.
Cancellation of the program was never the issue on the
C-5. They wanted to stay ignorant. If they had gotten the
facts, there was just no way they could have justified continuing the program. Particularly the technical facts. They
claim they couldn't understand the issue. The issue was
lying, cheating and stealing. . . . They don't want to listen;
debates have little or no value. I think they are unpre-
pared but I think for the most part they're victims of
self-programmed ignorance. There are exceptions of
course."

Two who Fitzgerald did not classify as exceptions were
Rep. Chet Holifield, Democrat from California, and Melvin Price, Democrat from Illinois, both of them chairmen
of subcommittees responsible for overseeing the Pentagon's
billion dollar spending programs.

Once Fitzgerald was asked by a House staffer to brief the
two lawmakers on the "should cost" approach to defense
contracts, a technique that Fitzgerald and others were pushing as a means of keeping defense contractors from inflating
their charges.

"It was like shouting into a vacuum. Price fell asleep and
Holifield was just sort of bland and nonresponsive."

How did the Defense Department regard its staunchest
supporters, like the House Armed Services Committee?

"It was a well-known fact in the Pentagon that they were
stooges. There were literally scripts written in the Pentagon
for many of the hearings, primarily on procurement stuff.

All during the C-5 debate, the entire procurement debate in the Senate, there was a speech-writing bureau set up in the Pentagon."

Fitzgerald also noticed that the military glamour and razzle-dazzle struck a responsive chord in many congressmen, both those who recalled their own experiences and those who fantasized on what might have been.

"I think people tend to romanticize their military experience. I can see why. I had a hell of a lot of fun in the service. The general public doesn't understand that it's a hell of a lot of fun . . . . The greatest compliment you could give them (the congressmen touring defense facilities) would be to dress them in a flight suit and helmet, put them in the cockpit and take their picture. They're so proud of that; they put it on their wall and everything. The military did it to the civilian officials at the Pentagon too, the assistant secretaries, deputies and everybody else. It's like an aircraft carrier. You cannot go on an aircraft carrier and see it in operation, the landings and takeoffs, without being tremendously impressed by the skill and bravery of the guys that do that. That may have nothing whatever to do with the wisdom of buying a plane but it affects your thinking. It's like the cavalry, they look good."

On the Vietnam War:

The way to have ended the war, says Fitzgerald, was to have made the American military accountable for it.

"Once we were into the damn thing you fire the generals that were unsuccessful, like Abraham Lincoln did. Say to all the bureaucrats, the military, industry and everyone else that there will be no promotions for generals until this is over, and we're going to get supertough on contracting, that there will be zero profits. Tell the troops in the field: no swimming pools, no beer every afternoon, you're here until it's over, like the way it was in the 'great war.' In other words, take all the profit out of the war for everyone, make it unattractive to everyone.

"Hell, without promotions the generals would have evacuated the troops right away. This business about the pitiful giant, and you can't lose face is a lot of crock. I think without promotions to the military and without profits to the industry they wouldn't say anything, they would just overtly stop favoring the war."

Fitzgerald doubts that the war was really as unpopular with the American majority as we might have thought. It was widely acclaimed a mistake but that was because it didn't work, it was a failure.

"If the war had been a brilliant military victory there wouldn't have been many voices against it. Now that doesn't make it any more moral, any more right.

"The only thing that was unpopular was the masses of infantry that were being killed. I told someone that when Nixon came in he would get the infantry out, because the army was sick of it. And there was no really big industry profit in the infantry business. The great bulk of explosives, ammunition (the stuff of a ground war) were from government owned contractor plants (GOCO's). The way it's being done now you make business for the aircraft manufacturers and the electronic people, the 'mic' (military industrial complex). An infantry war is not really good for them. Even though General Electric gets some Gatling gun orders, they get even more when we've got an air war."

A HOUSE CHRONOLOGY

NINETEEN SIXTY-THREE

Vietnam was not a burning issue in the House. Aside from the annual defense appropriations debate, the *Con-*

gressional Record turns up only one representative who expressed misgivings over what the United States was getting into.

"Mr. Speaker, a news item from this morning's *Wall Street Journal* notes the eightieth American boy to die in the fighting in South Vietnam. Why are American boys dying in a war the president refuses to call a war, yet commits our forces to it . . . ?

"What are we, the Congress, going to tell the American people as we stand by and allow American boys to be engaged in a war not declared by Congress? . . . By what right does President Kennedy commit armed forces to a continuing war without the sanction of Congress in accordance with the Constitution?"

The year's first and only on-the-record dove was Bruce Alger, an ultraconservative Republican from Dallas. Despite his fiery words of fidelity to the Constitution—words and principles which ultraliberals eventually would be voicing—Alger voted for the Gulf of Tonkin resolution the following year. Like many other conservatives, his traditional love for isolationism gave way to his ideological zeal for battling communists.

The defense appropriation debate in 1963 touched lightly on Vietnam—the $47 billion bill included funds for the growing number of helicopters being sent there—but Melvin Laird, then a member of the defense appropriations subcommittee, thought the Kennedy administration ought to dig itself in deeper.

"Perhaps worst of all," observed Laird, "we are trying to avoid the responsibilities of facing up to the communists in those areas where it has become crystal clear that we should face up to them, namely in Cuba, in Berlin, in Laos, in South Vietnam and in a number of other areas."

NINETEEN SIXTY-FOUR

The first presidential candidate to call for a U.S. military withdrawal from Vietnam was Eugene Siler.

Long before Eugene McCarthy or George McGovern ever dreamed of running as peace candidates, Siler, a Republican congressman from Kentucky, announced his availability and platform. The date was June 8, 1964. Siler had the good sense to issue his words of warning on the House floor, so they would be inscribed for immortality in the *Congressional Record*. He also had the good sense to be absent from the floor on August 7 of that year, the day the House voted 416 to 0 in favor of Lyndon Johnson's Gulf of Tonkin resolution. (Siler did send word, however, that he wanted to be paired against the measure and thus stands as the only representative recorded in opposition to the resolution. Adam Clayton Powell who said he was a pacifist showed up and voted "present." In the Senate, of course, Ernest Gruening and Wayne Morse notched their places in history by casting the only two "no" votes against the legislation that Johnson would later cite as his authority for waging war in Southeast Asia.)

Two months earlier Siler had taken to the floor during the one-minute speeches and had told his colleagues:

"I rise to announce my candidacy for president of the United States.

"I am running with the understanding that I will resign after twenty-four hours in the White House and let my vice-president take over the duties thereafter. Accordingly, I want an able and sufficient vice-president to run with me and then succeed me after that first day.

"What I propose to do in my day as president is to call home our 15,000 troops in South Vietnam and cancel our

part of that ill-fated, unnecessary and un-American campaign in Southeast Asia."

Siler proceeded to tick off in direct, mountaineer simplicity the reasons why the United States ought to leave Vietnam promptly: the war had been going on for nineteen
years, impervious to French and American attempts to end
it; George Washington had warned us to stay away from
foreign entanglements; the conflict was basically a civil war
between two totalitarian factions, one of which was communist controlled. If we were so intent on combating communism we need not go 6,878 miles to do so. Cuba was only
ninety miles away.

"This is my presidential one-day only platform," he concluded. "I would not be elected and very few will agree
with me, but this is the way I see it and I have said some
things that ought to be said by somebody."

NINETEEN SIXTY-FIVE

Nineteen sixty-five saw the United States begin bombing
of North Vietnam and commit its first ground troops to
combat in the South. Twenty-eight Democratic liberals
suggested to Chairman Thomas Morgan of the Foreign
Affairs Committe that maybe the time had come to hold
hearings on U.S. policy in Vietnam. Morgan, a personally
considerate man but not a visionary, politely rejected the
suggestion.

Mendel Rivers came to work fuming. The night before
he had seen a draft card burning protest on television. In
lightning fashion, he introduced a bill to make it a crime,

punishable by up to five years in prison and a $10,000 fine to knowingly destroy a draft card. That was on a Thursday. At its next scheduled meeting, a Monday, August 9, 1965, the Armed Services Committee approved the measure. The next day Rivers got unanimous consent to skip the usual waiting period and to bring the legislation directly to the floor. Following a brief debate, it passed 393 to 1. Henry Smith, a Republican from upstate New York, voted against the bill, telling reporters afterwards he thought five years in prison seemed a rather severe penalty. Three days later Senate Majority Leader Mike Mansfield brought the House-passed bill up in routine fashion. Sen. Strom Thurmond made a short speech in its behalf and the legislation was approved by voice vote. Both debates together took less than ten minutes.

The intent of the legislation was to punish those who opposed the war as well as the draft that fueled American participation in it. Rivers left no doubt about that when he told the House the bill was "a straightforward clear answer to those who would make a mockery of our efforts in South Vietnam by engaging in mass destruction of draft cards." It was left to William Bray, however, to fire the Armed Services Committee's big cannon. Bray was an Indiana Republican who fondly remembered his tank corps days in World War II.

"The need for this legislation is clear," he exclaimed. "Beatniks and so-called 'campus cults' have been publicly burning their draft cards to demonstrate their contempt for the United States and our resistance to communist takeovers. Such actions have been suggested and led by college professors, professors supported by the taxpayers' money."

So minuscule was the antiwar movement at the time, so darkly regarded were tactics of disruption that except for a few who were absent, all of the House's announced opponents of U.S. policy in Vietnam voted for the bill. They included such antiwar notables as Benjamin Rosenthal, Donald Fraser, Don Edwards, Robert Kastenmeier and self-proclaimed pacifist Adam Clayton Powell.

Nevertheless, men burned their cards, men were tried and convicted under the Rivers's amendment to the Selective Service Act and men went to prison. The Warren Supreme Court in 1968 upheld the constitutionality of the law by the surprisingly lopsided vote of 7 to 1. The Court held that Congress had a right to insure the effective working of the draft by enacting penalties for interference with it.

In retrospect it appears that its draft card decision marked one of the few times that the Warren Court came down on the wrong side of a civil liberties case. The justices failed to spot the freedom of expression issue, falling instead for the government's argument that Congress was attempting to assure efficient working of the system. In truth, the card played no part in the selective service system. During World War II, it was felt that issuance of the cards would help authorities nab draft dodgers. By 1965, few men carried them and no one was asked for them. A man either was or wasn't subject to the draft. Burning his card did not change his status. All it did was destroy a meaningless piece of paper.

One of the more interesting and least noticed developments of 1965 was the shaping of a Republican position on the war, a position that would be dusted off four years later and transformed into Richard Nixon's Vietnam policy.

GOP House members were in a tactical bind in 1965. Ideologically, the party supported the notion that America had "to put a stop to communist aggression"—which is what Lyndon Johnson was doing. At the same time, Republican strategists—such as Gerald Ford, the new leader,

Laird, and Charles Goodell, then the relatively conservative congressman from Upstate New York—felt Republicans ought to stake out their own approach to Vietnam, one
that would permit some criticism of the Democrats handling of the war. They decided to write a white paper on
Vietnam.

The document reflected the difficulty they were having.
Rather than hammer away at what was going on and what it
might lead to, it looked backward. It concluded that American troubles in Indochina stemmed from the mistakes of
former Democratic Presidents Truman, Kennedy and
Johnson. Only Eisenhower had acted wisely.

In a news conference, however, the Republican legislators sketched out a policy for the future. They would re-
peat it in the remaining years of the Johnson administration but without much gusto. Not surprisingly, the country
paid little attention to it.

"We fully support American personnel and their program in Vietnam. Make no mistake about that," Ford declared.

But he and the others added that they weren't pleased
with the way the war was being prosecuted. President Johnson was not fully utilizing America's enormous air and
naval superiority. The charge was not particularly original but no one else was doing much with the theme. One
who was was Richard Nixon, seemingly reassigned to the
permanent status of private citizen by two election defeats.

At the start of 1965 Nixon had proposed in a New York
City speech that the administration unleash the navy and
air force and let them carry the war to the supply lines and
staging areas in North Vietnam and Laos.

In 1966 the Republicans issued a second white paper on
Vietnam. This time they looked toward the future and
their prediction was grimly accurate: the war could take

five years to win and cost 125,000 American casualties. The nation, they said, must find a way to end the conflict "more speedily and at a smaller cost while safeguarding the independence and freedom of South Vietnam." No specific approaches were recommended in the paper, but at a news conference Laird et al, noted that the past December the Republican Coordinating Council—a policy-making group representing Republicans in and out of Congress—proposed using more planes and ships and fewer ground troops. One of the more influential members of the council was Laird, who presumably without realizing it, was helping to shape the military strategy that he and Nixon would employ when it came their turn to prosecute the war.

During his last days as House Minority Leader Gerald Ford looked back upon his unstinting support of America's military involvement in Indochina. He had no regrets and was sure as ever that his judgments were right.

"I don't think it was a mistake and history will indicate that. It was a proper commitment, first made by Mr. Truman and then by every president, in varying degrees, ever since. I think we made some mistakes in tactics and strategy but I don't think the fundamental objective was wrong, which is that the United States has to have a presence and influence world-wide in meeting the challenge of those that want to take over people or occupy territory, both for our own security and humanitarian reasons.. ..

"In Vietnam I think we should have more fully utilized air and sea power. Not committed ourselves as we did with ground forces. I happen to believe that if President Johnson had blockaded, which I had advocated, had used air power, which I advocated, at an earlier stage, some of our later problems would have been far less. I don't think we would have had to put 540,000 men into South Vietnam, as President Johnson did. I do think a different military strategy from 1962 through 1969 could have brought about a quicker end, less casualties, less cost than we did experience."

Charles Whalen of Dayton, Ohio, is also a Republican, but, unlike the overwhelming number of his colleagues, he did not follow the lead of Ford on the war. (Whalen says he was never pressured by Ford to join the team.) Instead he became one of the leaders in the House's antiwar movement. Because of the parliamentary advantages accruing at times to a member of the minority party, he played a key role. Whalen is polite and decent, and his decency is evident to just about everybody. That may be the reason few Republicans ever seemed to take him to task for opposing party and president. Most of them simply figured Whalen must have felt pretty deeply about the issue.

"When I came here in 1967 I knew virtually nothing about the Vietnam War, its roots, its origins. What brought about the change? Well, you grow, at least you hope you do. And I grew in a year-and-a-half. It started as a human thing.

"In April of 1967 we got a call to arrange for a funeral home, hotel and all that sort of thing, from a Dayton family whose son had been killed in Vietnam, and who was going to be buried in Arlington. I went down to the funeral home. The young fellow had been a student at the University of Dayton and I had known him as an ROTC graduate when I taught there. I paid my respects and condolence to the family. A sort of moment of truth came. For what purpose had he given his life? Fortunately I didn't have to answer the question then.

"It struck me as kind of sad. I go to funeral homes ten, maybe fifteen times a year. Young as well as old. This wasn't anything new to me. I don't want to overdramatize it. The family had two young children about seven and eight—they must have had a big gap—and an officer was pointing out the medals their brother had won. It impressed the kids. But I left and sort of dwelt on it. I did a lot of reading and soon had a whole shelf full of books.

"We would hear one story in the Armed Services Committee and then I would meet with other people—guys who had been in Vietnam, the press—and receive a completely different story. It was just evident to me we weren't getting the full story. In my reading I went all the way back to who got into Vietnam. At the time the question of the day was whether it was Kennedy, Johnson or Eisenhower. Well, it was Truman. I read Dean Acheson's book and he made that very clear. In 1950 or 1951 we were putting up a billion or more dollars to cover French military operations. We were seeking to perpetuate French colonialism and when that failed we set up our own colonialism. . . ."

By 1969, Whalen had decided to do what then was unthinkable for all but the most extreme antiwar Democrats—protest Vietnam policy by voting against the entire annual defense appropriation. At that time, it was virtually the only way for a House member to record his opposition to the war. But defenders of U.S. policy argued that a vote against the bill was a vote to abandon the "American boys" who had been sent to Indochina, to leave them helpless against the enemy.

"I figured, by God, a third of the bill is Vietnam, which means death and destruction and I just can't support it.

Reps. Donald Riegle and Paul McCloskey said, 'Oh, Chuck, you can't do that, you can't leave them stranded.' And I said, 'Well, we'll get 'em back somehow.' So I voted against the bill. It was my first one. It came late but there was a lot leading up to it. Afterwards I told people I would not vote for another defense appropriation bill as long as we were fighting in Vietnam, and I haven't."

NINETEEN SIXTY-SIX

The year opened with the House's tiny dove bloc bringing in outside experts and scholars to ponder Vietnam. When they were done, the participants concluded that the most productive course for the future was a deescalation of military activity. They offered a set of proposed settlement terms which included the securing of a cease fire; the establishment of a provisional form of rule, based on geographical control, to last until free elections could be held; international guarantees of the agreement and neutralization of the area. In short, the settlement, at least on paper, that Richard Nixon and Henry Kissinger worked out as a means of extricating the United States from Indochina. Not surprisingly, considering the standing of doves at the time, the House ignored the conference and recommendations.

The House preferred the future sketched for it by the Armed Services Committee. That panel sent over five members to survey the military situation in South Vietnam. The lawmakers had a nifty time. They put on battle fatigues and, as noted in their report to the guys back home, they "sat in with Enterprise pilots during their prestrike briefings, visited a number of Vietnamese hamlets with (marine) General (Lewis) Walt, went out on a river patrol operation with the navy and coast guard in the Mekong

Delta" and even visited "forward elements of the First Infantry Division during combat operations . . . and spent one night in the field. . . ." Exhilarated by the experience of battle, they told the House and the American people:

"Our forces have met the Vietcong and have mastered them in the field. We have demonstrated, after some painful starts, a typically American ability once again to outguess and outthink the enemy in his own brand of warfare . . . we feel it is already possible to see the light of 'victory' at the end of the tunnel."

That glimpse of sunshine a month earlier had prompted the House to approve a special $13 billion appropriation for the war. Only four members dared vote against the two bills providing the funds.

By anyone's yardstick but his own, Otis Pike is a mass of ideological contradictions. He steadfastly supported America's role in Vietnam while capitalizing on his Armed Services Committee membership to uncover and expose the unauthorized bombing of North Vietnam ordered by Gen. John Lavelle. He looks back with boyish delight on his World War II days as a Marine Corps fighter pilot; yet he took the lead in the House in attacking the Cheyenne helicopter and C-5 transport programs. To Pike there's nothing inconsistent in his positions. He says he judges each case on its merits. And because he is more intellectually honest and quicker of mind than most politicians he is able to turn that platitude into a reality. He has also been able to turn it into political success, carving out a reputation as a maverick. Since 1960 he has managed to convince enough Republicans and independents on easternmost, Republican Long

Island that they should elect a Democrat as their representative to the House.

In the House, Pike is respected by just about everyone
for his originality, intelligence and wit. He is not a man to
toy with in debate. But some of the promilitary people on
the Armed Services Committee can't understand how someone with Pike's brains, experience in the military and his
supposed affection for the American serviceman can be
critical so often of the Pentagon. To Pike the answer is
simple enough.

"My military experience has given me the confidence
which anybody needs to know that the military ain't perfect. I have seen the military waste so much with my own
eyes. I have seen them screw up so badly with my own eyes.
I have seen them be short of things which they desperately
needed and be long on things which they had no use for
whatsoever. I think that what it did for me more than anything else is give me the confidence in my own knowledge,
so that I don't hestitate to speak out because 'daddy knows
better.' "

That's the worthwhile side of a personal military experience. In an observation that goes a long way toward ex-
plaining the jingoism of many middle-aged House members during the Vietnam War, Pike also perceived a
disturbing political impact on the man who was thrust into
battle and emerged unscathed.

"Of course, one of the troubles with people of my generation is that for most of those who lived and got through the
war unwounded, it was a good experience. We went away
into an experience which was entirely lauded by our peers,
and we came home as heroes. And we wore our uniforms
proudly, and old ladies would get up and give us their seats
on the bus, this kind of stuff. And it was a very heady ex-

perience. And it was a good and on balance, exciting, pleasant experience. And this is probably very bad. Any time that war becomes a good experience for a whole generation of people, it is looked upon as a good solution for the international frustrations which any nation faces. And I think that that is what happened to my generation to a very large extent."

NINETEEN SIXTY-SEVEN

Ernest Fitzgerald thought the American people had supported the war—as long as we were winning it and not too many American lives were lost. That is arguable. What is less arguable is that winning or losing, Americans were not particularly anxious, in the opinion of most politicians, to pay for the war out of their own pockets.

In 1967 Lyndon Johnson decided he ought to ask Congress for some extra money to finance a conflict costing $20 billion to $30 billion a year. Johnson didn't exactly hide the reason for the 10 percent tax surcharge he was requesting but neither did he come right out and call it a war tax. Instead, he talked about the need to cool off the economy. It was the war against inflation rather than the war against the Vietnamese communists that took priority.

Many economists felt Johnson waited too long before asking for the tax increase and that the delay was one reason why inflation persisted so long after Vietnam expenditures had dropped sharply. Yet even after Johnson actually submitted his request it took Congress twelve months to enact the surcharge.

The House didn't duck all the difficult problems raised by the war. For example, it went after flag burners. It went after them with so much ardor that in passing a bill making the act a federal offense, punishable by up to a year in prison, it forgot to mention the word *burning*. It included defilement, defacement, mutilation and trampling. But its measure's chief sponsor, Rep. Jimmy Quillen of Tennessee, had been so excited at the prospect of realizing the first legislative success of his congressional career that in drafting the bill he left out the word "burning."

Nineteen sixty-seven ended with hawks still in firm control of the skies over the House. But signs of broad-based dissent were rumbling beneath the surface. Democrats who had been faithful to their president were now listening to their constituents or relying on their own judgment. In deference to Johnson, they would usually announce their break with the administration outside Washington. Here it would be picked up by the local press but not carried nationally where it could be added to similar pronouncements in other parts of the country.

In Cambridge, Massachusetts, Tip O'Neill responded to the pleas of his college-age daughters, caught up with his intellectual constituents and started leading his working class constituents away from the war. Morris Udall proclaimed his disillusionment in Arizona, where it would be less embarrassing to his brother, Stewart, Johnson's interior secretary. In Miami, Claude Pepper told a news conference that he could no longer support the military policy which he so loudly applauded during the Tonkin Gulf debate. And in northern California, Robert Leggett spent ten days during September touring his district and informing his constituents that the United States must sharply cut back its commitment to South Vietnam. A year earlier, Leggett had returned from South Vietnam with his four colleagues and signed the armed services subcommittee report which saw "victory" at the end of the tunnel.

NINETEEN SIXTY-EIGHT

The Tet Offensive, the toppling of Lyndon Johnson, record American war costs ($25 billion) and casualties (14,592 dead) turned 1968 into The Year of Vietnam for most of the country. Though not for Congress.

"There was not a single significant roll call taken on the Vietnam issue during the session," noted *Congressional Quarterly* in an end-of-the-year report.

In the Senate there was protracted debate over the war; in the House, not even that. During consideration of the defense appropriation bill, George Brown of California offered an amendment to prohibit further U.S. bombing of North Vietnam. Hawks were so firmly in command they did not bother to answer his arguments. As soon as Brown finished his speech, administration supporters called for a vote and the amendment was shouted down.

What the hawks in the House had going for them in 1968 —as they had in the previous years—was the enthusiastic backing of Speaker John McCormack, who could bring along the party loyalists and nonthinkers who populated the Democrats' rank-and-file. McCormack held a sincere, albeit simplistic belief in the rightness of the war. But he also went along because the two committees which handled war legislation—Appropriations and Armed Services—approved of it. And in McCormack's House, the Speaker always supported his committees. The tradition pleased committee chairmen; it infuriated many other Democrats.

Andy Jacobs came to the House in 1965, the son of a former congressman. He quickly distinguished himself as sensitive, joyous, irreverent and slightly eccentric. He felt desks took up too much space and were too pretentious, so he worked from a small table in the corner of his office. The saving left room for his Great Dane "C-5" ("He grew like a military contract.") which he frequently brought to work.

But there was also a highly sensitive side to Jacobs. He felt deeply, for example, about the war, about what he perceived as the House's refusal to face up to it. The support given the war by the Democratic leadership triumvirate—Speaker McCormack, Majority Leader Albert and Whip Boggs—turned the screw one more notch.

"I resented it, I really did. I felt the least they could have done was maybe not say anything one way or the other. I remember they had a big day on the floor a few years ago when Speaker McCormack came in and made this marvelous oration about how terrible the North Vietnamese were treating our prisoners, which I was persuaded at the time was accurate for him to say. But they didn't have to spend the whole afternoon saying what we already knew. After establishing the North Vietnamese were the wolves they might have gotten into the subject of who was responsible for throwing these kids to the wolves. But we never got around to discussing that, or whether it was necessary to throw them into a snake pit in the first place. So I was not inspired by such leadership.

"The way I read the Constitution the Congress is paid a salary to determine whether we should go to war. That's the way Abraham Lincoln read the Constitution. And therefore I don't think Congress is earning its money. They told me when we had our all night debate in 1969, before the moratorium, that it was the first time in the history of our participation in the Vietnam War that we had an honest-to-goodness discussion, rather than name-calling, in the House, where they really delved into it. It cannot be denied, regardless of how you came up on the issue, that the House shirked its responsibility to discuss it and to try to obtain information to find out, for example, whether paragraph six of the Geneva Accords of 1954 did create a national boundary."

Jacobs was bothered by something else about the House and Vietnam, what he saw as the indifference of many of its members to the suffering that the war was bringing to people, both Asians and Americans.

"Back in 1967 when the draft was up for a four-year extension somebody made a motion to cut the debate short. So when the college deferment amendment came up the limitation was sixty seconds a speaker. And that was all so that these guys could get over to the Paris Air Show, these guys who cared so much about 'our boys' and then used 'our boys' as political props in their campaigns. Sixty seconds to debate whether the draft should include college boys and boys from richer families. John Anderson took the floor and started describing the kinds of flowers blooming in Paris. It was one of the best speeches I heard in my life. It really put things precisely in perspective. It had underscored the callousness of being a hero on someone else's time. When I was nineteen years old and in Korea I had perceived then that most Americans looked upon war as a football game, that you go up to the Yalu River, you cross it, the whistle blows and you get six and then you kick for the extra point. People didn't really know that a bullet hurts. As Mr. Murrow said, 'The pain from the cut of a little finger would render more sensation to some people than the knowledge that their fellowman was being cut to ribbons somewhere else in the world.' "

NINETEEN SIXTY-NINE

It was Richard Nixon's war—to end, to fight or to withdraw from. He chose the last two.

The country and Congress waited for the unveiling of the Republican presidential candidate's "plan" for militarily disengaging the United States from Indochina. The plan turned out to be neither the quick, unilateral withdrawal sought by doves nor an attempt to win a decisive military victory, which hawks were calling for. Instead it was an amalgam of the old 1966 GOP air-and-sea power approach as well as a continuation and escalation of the Johnson administration's "de-Americanization" of the war, the gradual transfer of the fighting from United States to South Vietnamese forces. Nixon called it Vietnamization and looked to Melvin Laird, his newly appointed defense secretary and former House war strategist to successfully implement it.

The House was satisfied to give Nixon and Laird a chance. True, a few more Democrats had turned against the war now that the leader of their party had left the White House. But outspoken critics were still a minuscule minority. So minuscule in fact, that some Democrats felt a visceral need to fight the 1968 Chicago convention battle all over again and demonstrate to the country that Lyndon Johnson and they had been right about the war. As long as Richard Nixon continued what they perceived to be Johnson's policy he would receive their support.

Sometimes it came without Nixon asking. In the fall of 1969 Wayne Hays of Ohio and James Wright of Texas countered the October 15 "moratorium" against the war by drafting a resolution endorsing Nixon's policy. They won the quick and enthusiastic backing of Speaker McCormack, cleared it with the White House, picked up Republican cosponsorship and rushed it through the Foreign Affairs Committee and on to the floor.

On December 2, members marched lockstep and voted 333 to 55 in favor of the measure, which specifically ratified

Nixon's negotiating position and which implicitly approved his overall handling of the war. With a gleeful vengeance, representatives underscored the differences in House and Senate attitudes toward "backing our president." Democrats eagerly climbed aboard the bandwagon. Of the 226 who voted that afternoon, 172 lined up with the administration. (The only Republican to vote against Nixon was Ogden Reid of New York, who twenty-seven months later completed his process of alienation from the GOP by becoming a Democrat.)

NINETEEN SEVENTY

The hawks were still firmly in control. But major shifts of sentiment were taking place. The antiwar ranks in the House veritably tripled in size, growing from the fifty-five who had voted against the president on the Wright-Hays resolution in December 1969 to 153 who voted to halt the Cambodia operation seven months later. Most of the switching was taking place among Democrats. Blocs of big city northern liberals were voting overwhelmingly against the administration. Providing the bulk of Democratic support for the administration were southerners, most border state congressmen and the Democratic leadership. The votes of Speaker McCormack, Majority Leader Albert and Majority Whip Boggs represented more than three votes. Scores of Democrats without any deep personal convictions on the war watched their leaders for signals on how to vote.

To those in the House who felt deeply about the war, particularly those who opposed it, this indifference bordered on the criminal. During debate on the military procurement bill in May, Donald Riegle of Michigan became so infuriated at attempts to shut off debate on Vietnam amendments that he almost triggered a riot in the chamber. The youthful Riegle, steadily radicalized by the war, a week earlier had reached the point of moral exasperation with the invasion of Cambodia. When a majority of the House went along with Mendel Rivers and limited opponents to less than a minute apiece on pending amendments, Riegle exploded.

"What a sham," he shouted, speaking to the visitors' galleries. "I ask you, have you ever seen a worse sight in your life?"

Members, especially Republican members, sat up in their chairs and glowered at Riegle.

"For eight years, we have fought an undeclared war," he continued. "What can be more important than fully debating this issue? And where are those members who minutes ago voted to cut off debate? They're down in the House gym playing paddle ball."

With that bedlam broke out. Enraged Republicans leaped to their feet yelling, "No, no." Others screamed, "Point of order, point of order." The presiding member banged his gavel to restore order, and banged it again and again. Riegle could barely control himself. The offended Republicans were in a frenzy, their faces filled with hatred for this renegade member of the family that had embarrassed the House in public. Needless to say, it was never the same again for Riegle, and relations which already were straining broke down completely in 1973 when he quit the GOP and became a Democrat.

NINETEEN SEVENTY-ONE

Undoubtedly, this year was made to order for House doves. In March, House Democrats met in caucus and overwhelmingly went on record in favor of setting a legislative deadline for ending U.S. military activity in Indochina. A new procedural reform promised to make it much more difficult for members to duck a roll call vote on the war. Common Cause, the just-formed citizens' lobby, put withdrawal legislation at the top of its priority list and began developing a sophisticated constituent-to-congressman network to pressure the House into passing it. Events in South Vietnam, such as the one-candidate presidential election concocted by President Thieu, pained all but the most ardent hawks.

And finally, Senate Majority Leader Mike Mansfield devised the perfect antiwar amendment. It declared it to be "the policy of the United States" that all American military activities cease in Indochina within nine months (later six months), subject only to the release of American prisoners. The beauty of the proposal was that members could vote to establish a specific withdrawal date without having to cast the always-tough vote cutting off funds to the troops. The president would ignore the congressional declaration at his own risk and embarrassment, and certainly could no longer claim that Congress was backing his policy.

Yet with all this going for them, the doves failed again to enact withdrawal legislation. They came closer than ever before but in the end the House held fast for the president. The Senate passed the Mansfield amendment three times and three times the House rejected it. The closest the doves came to winning was on October 19, when the House beat back an attempt to attach it to the annual weapons procurement bill. The vote was 215 to 193, with several hawks voting with the doves for tactical reasons in a confused parliamentary situation.

A switch of only eleven members would have put Congress on record against the war and would have proclaimed unilateral American withdrawal as national policy. As it turned out, President Nixon was able to conclude U.S. military participation in Vietnam on his terms, rather than the Senate's. The end came nineteen months after the House first failed to pass the Mansfield amendment and fifteen months after the unsuccessful October try.

NINETEEN SEVENTY-TWO

Doves were within striking distance. They had the momentum. Election year consciousness had combined with growing war weariness throughout the country. Widescale defections from the administration were expected.

Antiwar forces got off to a fast start. The liberal Democratic Study Group fashioned a strategy aimed at preventing powerful or well-placed Democratic holdouts from thwarting the will of their antiadministration colleagues. Common Cause designated the House and the war as its prime target for the year.

On April 20 the Democratic caucus overwhelmingly approved a resolution directing—not asking or urging, but directing—Democrats on the Foreign Affairs Committee to draft end-the-war legislation and get it to the floor promptly. So decisive and widespread was the sentiment in favor of the caucus measure that even Speaker Albert and Majority Leader Boggs reluctantly felt compelled to join in making up the two-to-one margin of victory.

Three months later the committee's loyalist Democrats overcame the opposition of most of the panel's Republicans as well as a handful of Democratic cold warriors and complied with the caucus directive. It tacked on to the annual foreign aid authorization an amendment mandating a halt to U.S. military activity in or over Indochina by October 1, conditioned only upon release of prisoners, an accounting of the missing and a limited ceasefire to the extent necessary to carry out the withdrawal. (President Nixon wanted a full-fledged cease fire.)

On August 10 the House knocked the amendment out of the bill. The roll call vote was 229 to 177. It wasn't only the margin that embittered Democratic war foes. Sponsor of the motion to kill the Vietnam amendment was longtime liberal reformer Richard Bolling, whose iconoclastic brilliance included a stern willingness to face down the communists abroad. Among the eighty Democrats voting with the administration were Democratic Leaders Albert and Boggs.

What happened to the doves' dreams of success? They were dashed by events on the battlefield in Vietnam and in the political arena at home. President Nixon's counter response to the North Vietnamese spring offensive—his mining of Haiphong Harbor and heavy bombing of the North —struck a responsive and favorable chord with millions of Americans. No longer was the war a dreary and costly deadlock with no end in sight. The president had taken the initiative, they felt, and might well bomb the communists into accepting United States peace terms. A Louis Harris poll taken at the end of August showed a substantial majority endorsing the president's course of action. House members spotted that upsurge of support for Nixon and reacted accordingly. Defections were checked; some conservative opponents of Nixon's "no-win" policy returned to the fold.

Common Cause lobbyist Fred Wertheimer offered another reason: the nomination of George McGovern. It alienated many Democrats; the Eagleton disaster that followed demoralized the rest. By midsummer, in Wertheimer's view, any House member worth his salt had concluded Nixon was going to win in a walk and that Vietnam was not going to be a crucial issue with the voters. He or she could safely back the president on the war without fear of reprisals at home.

NINETEEN SEVENTY-THREE

"Ten . . . nine . . . eight . . ." The crowd chanted the countdown as the digital clock ticked off the remaining seconds. A roar went up when the clock hit double zeros.

The scene was not a basketball game. It took place on the floor of the House of Representatives. The "crowd" was a knot of Democratic doves following the tally on the House's new electronic voting system.

The date was May 10, 1973. After nine years of mulling it over, the House of Representatives had cast its first vote ever against the war in Indochina.

The cheering by the doves was more playful than passionate. Maybe that was because the vote came three and a half months after a cease-fire had been proclaimed in Vietnam and after the last American troop had been withdrawn from the south and the last POW brought home from the North. To most Americans the war was over and Vietnam behind us. They were ready for passage of antiwar legislation. Speaker Albert voted for it.

Yet the vote on May 10, and the series of antiwar votes that followed it over the next seven weeks, proved to be far more crucial than the doves realized. The United States may have been militarily disengaging itself from Indochina, but what happened in Congress, and particularly in the House, made sure that it would not go back.

Congress and the president ended America's direct military role in the war in a welter of confusion, misunderstanding, surprise and irony. And perhaps by accident.

On May 10 the House voted 219 to 188 to stop the U.S. bombing of Cambodia. Henry Kissinger and Le Duc Tho had been unable to settle the conflict in that country, and the Nixon administration was determined that it not fall to the communists. Thus the daily air attacks.

Following the May 10 vote, the Senate began adding on the Cambodia amendment—which was broadened to include a bar against resuming the bombing of Laos—to every vulnerable bill in sight, meaning every piece of legislation the president would have a hard time vetoing. By June 29 the list included the debt ceiling bill, a continuing appropriation resolution and a supplemental money bill. The first two were absolutely essential. If the debt bill was not enacted by July 1, the government could no longer borrow money, an infirmity that would throw the securities market in particular and the financial community in general into chaos. Failure to approve the continuing appropriation by July 1 could soon bring chaos to the government, its major departments and agencies deprived of any authority to spend money in the new fiscal year.

But doves were adamant. The time had come to say no. Hadn't "peace with honor" been declared on January 27? What legal, moral or political justification was there for further U.S. military involvement in the region? That was that. The president would either accept the amendment or accept the consequences.

The president was just as firm. A total halt to U.S. air operations in Cambodia would virtually remove any pressure on the communists there to negotiate a settlement, risk a communist military takeover in the country and endanger the regional-wide peace outlined by Henry Kissinger and the North Vietnamese.

So high were the stakes, said presidential adviser Melvin Laird, that Nixon would veto every bill that came to him with an immediate Cambodia bombing cutoff provision.

Following the first such veto, Senate Democratic Leader Mike Mansfield vowed that the Senate would attach the amendment to every piece of legislation "over and over again," until the will of the people prevailed and until the president recognized which branch had been assigned the war-making powers by the Constitution.

"If the president doesn't want to stop the bombing but does want to stop the government, that's his business," Mansfield said angrily.

"We're eyeball to eyeball in a historic confrontation," warned Rep. Robert Giaimo, a leader of the House anti-war forces.

The president blinked first. He let it be known that he would accept a cutoff if it was pushed back to August 15. In one sense, the proposal worked in Nixon's behalf. It split apart the dove bloc. Some saw it as a means of finally getting a termination-of-hostilities deadline into law. Others, however, denounced it as morally repugnant because it permitted Nixon to bomb and kill for an extra forty-five days. They also saw it as a cowardly surrender by Congress to the president.

The battle was joined on the afternoon of June 29. Over the protests of holdout doves, the House accepted the compromise. But what neither opponents or supporters realized at the time was that the amendment adopted went further than the administration had intended or than the doves had demanded.

The House had tacked on to the supplemental appropriation bill an amendment that would bar U.S. combat activities over not only Cambodia and Laos but over North and South Vietnam as well. The press and most members paid scant attention to this last minute addition of Vietnam. Cambodia was the location where the fighting was taking place, not Vietnam, where a ceasefire had been proclaimed. It was U.S. bombing of Cambodia that Congress was trying to stop.

Administration officials, however, took note of the change and reacted with alarm. From the point of view of Nixon policy, their shock was understandable. It was one thing for the president to sign away his claimed constitutional right to unilaterally intervene in Cambodia or Laos. It was another thing entirely to give up on South Vietnam. To accept legislation prohibiting him from immediately responding to a communist military move in the south would, in the rhetoric of the administration, be inviting aggression from the north. It would run counter to everything Nixon had been saying and doing in Vietnam over the past four years. Yet that is precisely what he agreed to. That agreement was not willingly given. Nixon did not realize the full implications of what was taking place on the House floor until it was too late to do anything about it. Lapses of that sort were uncharacteristic of Nixon. In retrospect, it might be explained by his growing preoccupation with Watergate.

Watergate also leads us to speculate on what Nixon might have done had he been armed with what he considered his authority to return to Vietnam during the final days of his presidency. Analysts will tell us that even without a congressional prohibition blocking him from action, Nixon would have had to take leave of his political senses to resume bombing North Vietnam. But how inconceivable is it to imagine that Nixon could have taken leave of his senses, that pushed by the final agonies of Watergate an irrational president would view a "bold" move in Vietnam as a means of diverting public attention from his domestic tragedy? Or perhaps, acting less cynically, he would relieve his inner torment by lashing out at the communists in place of retaliating against his critics? The speculation may be idle, but it seems obvious that we were better off in 1974 with Richard Nixon barred from committing U.S. military forces to Indochina.

One of the principal participants in the events that led to enactment of the Vietnam prohibition was Nixon's successor. House GOP Leader Gerald Ford served as the administration's spokesman during the House debate. It was he who shuttled back and forth between the House floor and a phone booth in the House Republican cloakroom where he spoke with Nixon, White House Chief of Staff Alexander Haig and presidential adviser Melvin Laird at San Clemente. At one point Ford was forced to call Nixon and get personal assurances from the president that he regarded August 15 as a hard, fast and legal deadline, an assurance he relayed to the House. What Ford did not convey to his colleagues was his discovery that Nixon and some of his aides were less concerned about the date than they were about the inclusion of Vietnam in the prohibition. A week afterwards, sitting in his Capitol office, Ford confided how spontaneous and unplanned—as well as contrary to the president's position—that concession was.

"On the night before the Cambodia vote, I wrote down three points I was going to make. Number one, Nixon would accept August 15 as a bombing deadline. Number two, the ban on U.S. military activities would apply to all of Southeast Asia. And number three, the president would veto any legislative deadline earlier than August 15.

"Two members of the White House staff, one from Department of Defense, were here and I read the three points to them the night before. I read to them what I was going to say. The next morning they were here very early—eight, eight-thirty, I don't know, something like that—I reread it to them because I wanted specific reconfirmation. I had the feeling they didn't quite understand the significance of the words 'all of Southeast Asia' but I had written it down on a piece of paper which is now in my scrapbook.

"I made my floor speech, following Appropriation's Committee Chairman George Mahon's speech. At that point, White House lobbyist Max Friedersdorf, Pentagon legislative chief Jack Marsh and somebody else from the White House got me off the floor and said, 'Oh, Jerry, you can't say Southeast Asia, you've got to limit it to Cambodia.' I said to them, 'I have said it on the floor, you confirmed it and reconfirmed it and there's no way to go back on it. Sorry, that's it, period.' They said, 'It can't be that way.' I said, 'I'm sorry.'

"So I went back to the floor and the debate went on and on and on. My colloquies on the floor (on whether Ford's proposed compromise had presidential sanction) took place. I said, 'No, I didn't talk to the president but to White House sources.' And at that point there was some laughter or booing or whatever it was. Apparently Friedersdorf and his associates were in the gallery and they felt that things were deteriorating a bit. Maybe they were. So they called Timmons. Timmons called the White House (in San Clemente) and the president then called me. I took the call in the Republican cloakroom off the House floor. I talked to the president for about ten minutes. I read to him the three points I made on the House floor and he said, 'That's fine.' Then I went back on the floor and I reconfirmed what I had previously said and told the House that the president approved of it.

"Five minutes later or so I got a call from Al Haig. He

said, 'Oh, you can't do that. The president won't accept it.' I said, 'Al, it's done. That's it. I'm sorry but there's no way I can erase what I said. It is my understanding that this is what the president approved in his conversation with me.' Al was obviously disappointed. He said, 'I was sitting in the room with the president when you talked to the president. What you have said was apparently not what the president understood you to have said.' I said, 'I'm sorry, Al, but that's the way it has to be.' About five minutes later, maybe ten minutes, I got a call from Mel Laird, out at San Clemente. Mel said, 'Everything's okay. Don't worry about it.' That's it. I never asked Mel. But I can't help but believe that the president called Mel in and Mel and the president and Al Haig talked about it. It was my impression that the three of them then decided that what I had said on the floor had their approval. Because in the meantime there was a big hassle on the Senate side as to whether it should be limited to Cambodia or broadened to include Southeast Asia. Apparently my comment on the floor of the House resolved that problem in the Senate. That's what I'm told.

"I wrote down what I thought had to be said to win. In retrospect they say they didn't understand what I was saying. I thought it was pretty clear. Without it I think we might have gotten through. But it would have been a hard fight and I'm not sure the Senate would have taken just Cambodia. I think we might have won in the House.

"I don't like to put it on the basis of win or lose but I thought we made a very successful compromise. It was not all we wanted, but enough to give Henry Kissinger a chance to achieve what they thought could be accomplished in Cambodia. And I really, in retrospect, honestly believe that if we hadn't put in Southeast Asia the end result would have been chaos. The Cambodian provision was a rider to an appropriation bill that involved funding for a lot of agencies of the federal government. We could have had a very, very difficult situation if the bill had been vetoed."

WHAT DIFFERENCE DID IT MAKE?

The House's refusal to repudiate the war until 1973 probably prolonged American military involvement in Indochina by one to two years. During that time between 300 and 1,000 American servicemen were killed, between approximately 580 and 2,950 were wounded and between 315 to 358 were captured or reported missing in action.

The impact on Indochina itself of an earlier unilateral United States withdrawal would have been enormous. Obviously, the Thieu government would not have been as well prepared to face off against the communists as it was on January 27, 1973, having had the additional time to build its own military strength. An earlier American departure might have led to a communist takeover by 1973. But whether such a scenario would have led to more or less death and destruction than that which has occurred since mid-1971 is of course something we will never know.

WHY DID THE HOUSE HOLD ON?

Doves like Ben Rosenthal maintained through the final years of the war that the House lagged behind the people in its stand on Vietnam. Only the Senate accurately reflected national sentiment. I'm not so sure. Rosenthal's district in Queens was overwhelmingly against the war. Sam Stratton's in Upstate New York apparently was not. Or if it was, it didn't seem to bother his constituents that Stratton never wavered in his tough, vocal defense of U.S. policy in Indochina. White House lobbyist Richard Cook maintained that while senators and their staffs were reading the

Washington Post, The New York Times and the big metropolitan newspapers in their states—the ones generally opposed to the war—House members were reading and learning from the small dailies in their districts, the ones that more often than not either supported U.S. actions in Southeast Asia or if they didn't, at least didn't make too much of a fuss over it.

Polls taken at the time were relatively useless. They went both ways, depending on how the war was going at the time, how forceful the president appeared. Interestingly, a poll commissioned by an antiwar group in 1970 disclosed that many people who said they favored a U.S. pullout were unaware that their representatives had been regularly voting to keep the troops there.

While we'll never know whether the House followed or disregarded the national mood on the war during 1971 and 1972—the years when a switch by the House could have led to a congressionally forced withdrawal—we do know that the House did not lead the people or mold opinion. Rather, its rank and file, particularly the Democratic hacks, decided that when it came to Vietnam, and military matters in general, it would stick with its leaders, like John McCormack.

And as McCormack often said, when it came to matters of defense, he would start off on the premise that it was best to err on the side of strength. And if he still had doubts, he would follow the lead of men like Mendel Rivers.

And Mendel Rivers was never known as a man who believed in keeping the military on a tight leash.

"We can beat anyone," he remarked in 1965. "Some are more concerned about escalation in Vietnam than victory. I'm not."

10

Some Modest Proposals

AFTER OBSERVING the House closely for twelve years I have concluded, with shining ambivalence, there is much that is wrong with the House and much that is right about it. Unfortunately for the House, as well as for the rest of us, the negative qualities usually win out. The positive features end up being described as the House's marvelous "potential."

And the potential is great. The Judiciary Committee's televised impeachment performance was a classic example. Over and over I heard from people who had little previous. contact with the House how pleasantly surprised they were to discover so many members who were articulate, thoughtful, diligent and colorful. The committee contained a few out-and-out hacks, a somewhat larger group which achieved the status of mediocre, a plurality of competent but unexceptional legislators and a few outstanding individuals. I think it's fair to say the Judiciary Committee served as a cross section of the House.

It's not only in Washington that representatives can fulfill their potential. Because they have less territory and population to worry about, because they are less recognizable and because they are more accessible to ordinary people, House members can develop a better feel for their constituents than senators can about theirs. If they want to, men and women of the House can truly fulfill their theoretical role as the reflection of the national mood and will.

The structure of the House—the rules it follows, the system under which it operates—is largely sound. But it has traditions—as opposed to rules—which are debilitating and the major cause of its weakness today. Offhand I can think of only one or two changes in the House rules that cry out for immediate change.

What is wrong with the House are the people who run it, and the traditions that permit them to assume power. Sometimes they are the best; more often they are not. Frequently they are people who are past their prime. It becomes a matter of luck whether party leaders are individuals who provide imaginative and strong, vibrant leadership. And if the leaders of the majority party are uninspiring, the House will be uninspiring. The same elements of chance apply to subcommittees and committees, where the quality of chairmen will often determine the quality of the legislative product sent to the floor and passed by the House.

With chairmen, it's the seniority tradition that does the damage. Hang around long enough on the same committee and the inevitability of death and retirement or defeat at the polls will eliminate enough of those above to move you into a chairmanship. Much has been said and written about the destruction that seniority has left in its path.

With leaders, especially the Democratic ones, it is the "ladder" tradition which is the culprit. The majority leader succeeds the Speaker and the whip succeeds the majority leader. From Rayburn to McCormack to Albert. Had not majority leader and one-time whip Hale Boggs been killed in a 1972 plane crash, he would be the heir apparent today. Instead it is Majority Leader Thomas O'Neill who moved up from whip to majority leader. Mavericks have tried to break the ladder sequence but their fellow Democrats have soundly rebuffed them.

Individuals grow with service and experience. But only up to a point. At a certain age the curve slopes downward. At seventy, the age he was when he became Speaker, John McCormack was not the man he was at forty, when he became majority leader. At the age of forty-seven, Carl Albert possessed a multitude of leadership qualities. Because he did, Sam Rayburn tapped him for the job of whip in 1955. Sixteen years later, nine of them spent as the loyal lieutenant to McCormack, a less qualified Albert became Speaker.

The result of both the tradition and the trend is that the House has turned into an uninspiring legislative center. It has ratified and tinkered with what presidents have proposed but has done little creative legislating on its own. It has failed dismally at its oversight responsibilities, leaving government agencies to distort and sometimes ignore the spirit behind the laws they are supposed to implement.

WHAT CAN BE DONE ABOUT THE HOUSE?

The internal rules of the institution are generally sound. It isn't easy to devise a method by which a body with 435 members can act in a democratic fashion and get things done. The House rules pretty much achieve that goal. I would make two changes. One deals with the Rules Committee, which has been a pest to speakers and presidents for years. Its wings have been clipped but it can still be troublesome and block the House from working its will. Simply put, the Rules Committee should be limited strictly to doing what it was supposed to do, namely, control the flow of legislation to the floor. Its members should not be allowed to decide whether they like or dislike a bill and be empowered to keep a measure from the floor. The committee should be authorized solely to recommend to the House the ground rules for debating the bill. If it balks at acting, its favorite device of obstruction, the bill should be called up by the leadership and debated under prescribed rules for such situations or under rules set at the time by the House.

The other change I would like to see is a streamlining of debate itself. Much of the House's so-called general debate —that period when the bill can be talked about but not amended—is wholly unnecessary. Each week dozens of hours are wasted as members of the committee reporting the bill deliver lengthy monologues to near empty chambers. Yet during the meaningful part of the debate, when amendments are considered, a member is normally limited to five minutes for each amendment. And when a majority of the House gets impatient, the limitation can be cut even further, creating situations where members literally are given thirty seconds to propound their views. It would be relatively simple to revise the rules and sharply cut back the time allotted for general debate. Some of the savings could be applied to the amending process, perhaps boosting the individual speaking limit from five to ten minutes.

But as I have said, rules do not constitute the House's major problems. People do. The wrong people placed in key positions by the seniority and ladder traditions. Good people below—and there are many good, terribly hardworking people, eloquent people in the House—are being smothered or bored or both. For years reformers inside and outside the House have tried to modify both traditions. They've racked up a few successes but by and large they have not gotten to the heart of the problem. My own view is that only a drastic remedy will work. An analogy is that of an icebound river. In order to get the waters flowing again the ice has to be blasted apart, not chipped away.

The explosive I have in mind to unclog the House is a constitutional amendment limiting members to eight years of service. Enough time to learn something about government and apply that knowledge as a legislator.

What the House needs desperately is turnover. It needs new people who will offer new ideas. It needs people who will maintain the same level of excitement at the end of their service in the House as they did when they entered it.

Now, the eager and innovative member sits and waits. Eventually he reaches a position of responsibility and for a few years he can give much to the job. But more often than not he goes downhill. There are exceptions but far too many House members allow themselves to become bureaucratized by the job. They may work long, difficult hours. They may remain conscientious public servants. But they become careerists instead of representatives. They plod through the same basic authorization or appropriation process year after year. In 1974, a great number of members chose to retire. Many of them said they were leaving because the job wasn't fun anymore. Well, who has ever said that it was supposed to be fun?

I rather doubt that the founders envisioned men making a lifetime career of the House, remaining there for thirty, forty and even fifty years. They certainly didn't expect seniority to be the criterion for selecting leaders. The late George Galloway, in his *History of the United States House of Representatives,* noted that before 1896 the men averaged only seven years of service in the House, and that Henry Clay and William Pennington were elected as freshmen.

One of the reasons members are staying longer and

longer—to the point where the membership's average age now tops by many years the average age of the electorate— is that the job itself has become too personally attractive. Not only the salary, but the trappings of the position, the fringe benefits, the handsome retirement plan end up constituting a sort of conflict of interest with the member's representative responsibilities. He continues in the job not necessarily because he is that fond of legislating but because he has too much invested in it to quit. After ten or fifteen years away from his profession, he is no longer sure he can do as well back home for himself and his family as he can by staying in Congress.

Limiting a member to eight years of service will guarantee constant turnover in the membership. The issues of seniority and leadership ascension would become moot. A less entrenched House membership would be unlikely to tolerate the ladder system. Seniority could continue. It has always had virtue of fairness and objectivity. Its flaw is that it risks installing people in chairmanships far longer than they belong there. By forcing a member to leave after eight years, that danger is virtually wiped out.

Along with limiting representatives to four terms, I would eliminate all fringe benefits and do away with all allowances except those that enhance a member's ability to serve his constituents. Abolish the pension plan. Shut down the private dining rooms. Cut back the Capitol police force. Make members live like the rest of us. Let them know something of the every day inconveniences the rest of us put up with. Filling the position of a congressman should represent a period of service to the country, a period that many people would find stimulating and challenging.

If service in the House is a privilege, as members are forever telling their constituents, they should be more than willing to permit others in their districts to share that privilege by voting for the necessary constitutional amendment and sending it along to the states for their ratification. Obviously, that is not going to happen. House members with years of seniority, or those looking forward to years of seniority, are not about to voluntarily vote themselves out of a job. But that does not mean they cannot be pressured into doing so. In recent years outside groups have forced House members to disclose the source of their campaign money, reveal some of their personal financial holdings and enact procedural reforms they would just as soon have rejected. The idea of limiting House members to four terms in office is one which the public could easily comprehend, and support enthusiastically. Pushed by citizen groups like Common Cause and the League of Women Voters, the concept could catch on. Candidates for the House could pledge to vote for such a constitutional amendment and challenge the incumbent to do the same.

The expected immediate objection to the limitation is that the House would suffer from inexperience, would lose the benefits of those who had developed a specialization in a particular field. It was the argument advanced in 1787 when delegates to the Constitutional Convention omitted from the new Constitution that provision in the Articles of Confederation which barred members of the Continental Congress from immediately running for reelection. Under the provision, James Madison had to step aside. The danger does exist that under the eight-year limitation the country will be deprived of another James Madison.* But by the same token the present system may be now depriving us of another James Madison, someone with ster-

---

* Besides being the period we limit our presidents to, eight years (from 1789 to 1797) constituted Madison's service in the House.

ling talents who either was blocked from getting into Congress or from moving up to positions of influence while at the peak of his or her abilities. I'm convinced the net result would be beneficial.

It is also the belief of a growing number of thinkers that we have overrated the need for specialization in many fields or that we have overestimated the duration of service required to achieve it. Some have even suggested that individuals in white collar professions regularly change fields or careers after a number of years. They contend it benefits both the institution involved and the individuals. R. Sargent Shriver, first director of the Peace Corps, persuaded Congress to enact five-year limitations on the length of time professionals could serve in the agency. Shriver felt the way to keep both agencies, the Peace Corps and the Office of Economic Opportunity, faithful to their innovative spirit was to prevent their bureaucratization. Many members and staff aides in Congress now have demonstrated that they can quickly master a variety of subjects.

In the event a constitutional amendment is adopted, what do we do with the members already in the House? Do we include a grandfather clause? That would exempt present members and could delay full implementation of the plan for years. Perhaps like industries seeking to automate against union resistance, we'll have to promise the incumbents full pensions immediately if they will quit now. Perhaps public acceptance of the idea will induce many to depart gracefully and voluntarily.

Finally, what do we do about the Senate? My inclination is to leave it alone for the time being, if for no other reason than to reassure those who fear that constant turnover at the Capitol will bring about uncontrollable turmoil and the collapse of the Republic. While the House stood for innovation, the Senate could represent stability. After observing how the change worked in the House, the country could then think about applying it to the Senate. Our first task, however, is to transform the House from a House *for* Representatives back to a House *of* Representatives.

INDEX